Cinema
Architecture

Cinema Architecture

Chris van Uffelen

BRAUN

CONTENTS

Multi-focus

Customer-focus

REX

"Cinema should make you forget you are sitting in a theater." (Roman Polanski)

by Chris van Uffelen

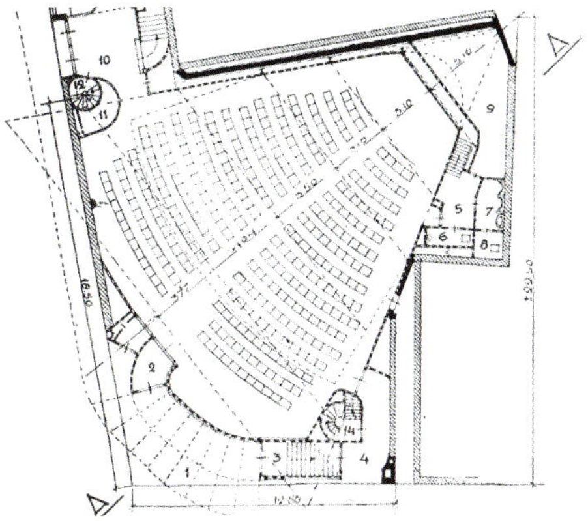

↑ | **Émile Reynaud,** Praxinoscope, 1882: A predecessor of cinema since 1877
↑↑ | **Jan Duiler,** 1 Cineac, amsterdam, 1934: News cinema in rational structure
↖↖ | **Hijman Louis de Jong,** Tusschinsky, Amsterdam, 1921: Giant lamp in theater-like and luxurious auditorium
↖ | **Auguste Bluysen and John Eberson,** Rex, Paris, 1932: Art Déco
←← | **Adrien Fainsilber,** La Géode, Paris, 1985: omnimax theater in the form of a sphere
← | **Valode & Pistre Architects,** UGC-Cinema Bercy Village, Paris, 1998: Cinema renewing the urban fabric

Cinema buildings – in the strictest sense, this connotes the structure surrounding a screen, projection equipment and an auditorium. The history of cinema architecture began with the use of existing buildings for purposes beyond their original intent. Early films were presented in private homes and cafés (Thomas Edison 1891, Lumiére brothers 1895). When silent movies first emerged, they were shown in ballrooms and music halls, and during the first decade of the 20th century simple stores were also used in working class neighborhoods. At this time already, "cinemas" took over the concept of the picture stage from theater architecture (a stage with a portal frame opening towards the audience). This architectural similarity continued to be applied when independent film theaters started to be established, starting approximately in 1910. Since theaters and cinemas had to provide similar usage structures, their designs were often closely related, except that in movie theaters the stage area and scenery were only present in a very basic form or could be eliminated altogether. At this time, screens were frequently extricable, as the movie presentation was sometimes only part of a much more extensive evening entertainment program. Stage presentations, such as ballet and vaudeville, complemented the films. As early as 1908, two to three million people in the U.S. visited movie theaters daily, and the new medium, an inexpensive "Nickelodeon" (with an entrance fee of five cents) soon replaced dime novels as the primary form of simple entertainment of the masses. During the World War I, "atmosphere theaters" emerged in the U.S. and competed with regular theaters. Their opulent decoration of sceneries that seem to stem from the movies themselves were the first form of movie theater interior design. In Europe, cinemas increasingly sought to establish an independent identity, which turned out to be pompously luscious. While theaters frequently continued to be built in the neo-Baroque style of the Paris Opera by Charles Garnier (1875), cinemas adopted a fairly-tale opulent style (Hijman Louis de Jong: Tuschinsky, Amsterdam, 1921, with a remnant of the stage and the organ). At the same time, their architecture continued to emulate the prestigious style of theater buildings with rounded galleries, boxes and foyers. These two tendencies – the continuation of the structural concept and the change in style – were further amplified by the introduction of sound films (with ascending auditoriums as of 1928) and Art Déco was established as the typical interior style of increasingly large movie theaters (Auguste Bluysen and John Eberson: Rex, Paris, 1932, with scenery by Maurice Dufrêne, 3,300 seats). At the same time, buildings dedicated to the modern style, such as Erich Mendelsohn's Universum in Berlin (1928, semicircular street side, crowned by a tall venting shaft) were established before World War II. For example, in Amsterdam across from the ostentatious ceramics façade of the Tusschinsky the radically sober white modern Cineac by Jan Duiker (1934) can be found, a news cinema without fixed presentation times, that had to cope with constant audience admittance and exiting.

In case of several performances in one evening, guiding the audience was and continues to be a key problem for movie theaters. The entering and exiting streams of visitors have to be led past each other, while escape routes are extremely important, given the highly flammable nature of film materials. A further problem is climate control, especially air conditioning. In the Tusschinsky already, a sophisticated duct and air passage system was developed involving a room in which new blocks of ice were deposited on a daily basis. The cinematograph (Greek: kinematos and grápho: image writer) permanently altered society in the first half of the 20th century. It not only signified the transition from static pictures to the reproduction of moving objects, but it simultaneously developed into a new form of mass media (Walter Benjamin: The Work of Art in the Age of Mechanical Reproduction, 1936). The interest of the arts in movement (serial photography by E. Muybridge and its acceptance among the Impressionists) was fulfilled within a short period of time and new forms of reality presentation and alteration were found (the technical enthusiasm of the Futurists, kinetic art), incorporating time and space into the presentation (cut, camera tracking, spatialization of time, temporalization of space, Erwin Panofsky: Style and Medium in the Motion Pictures, 1934).

Following World War II, cinema buildings continued the modernist trend in architecture and the media theory of movies, with a much more humble daytime appearance than the previous movie palaces. In the evenings, however, they shone brightly with flamboyant fluorescent letters, literally outshining the competing theaters. The interior increasingly focused on comfort – arm chairs and abstract decoration such as crimped walls dominated the appearance. At the same time, the opulent decorations disappeared and the auditorium and projection area increasingly developed into an "invisible cinema" in which nothing should distract from the film and in which the setting should not reflect on the action of the film. The Black Box of the auditorium symbolizes the head of the director with whose eyes the audience should experience the events of the movie as conveyed by the screen. However, at this time, the zenith of post-war movies had already passed. During the 1960s, many of the large movie theaters were torn down and large auditoriums, in which attending a movie had the feel of a community event, were split into several small theaters.

Finally, during the 1970s and 1980s, cinemas started to compete with television, becoming part of a general leisure culture, losing their status as an exclusive evening entertainment venue, and were accordingly increasingly incorporated into multifunctional buildings. To compete with television, the 70-mm film was developed, as well as the wide screen formats (1:1.66, 1:1.85,) and Scope (1:2.35, 1:2.55), which laterally "overstrain" the human eye (1:1.54) pulling the observer deeper into the happenings on screen. These wide screens also required the new construction or restructuring of existing cinemas. During the 1990s, cinema centers were established, often operated by national or international chains, which attempted to reestablish the cinema as an evening-filling program – complementing the film presentation, bars and restaurants offer an extended leisure program. Cultural centers and buildings (museums, exhibition halls) also became increasingly involved in the movie culture, offering independent movie showings or including film art as part of their exhibitions. In contrast to the cinema center in the downtown area of cities, large cinema complexes were also established at the fringe of cities, usually within the context of shopping malls. These are easily accessible from the city as well as surrounding areas, offering more focused leisure activities, which are usually "wildly distributed" within the city – shopping, fitness and wellness are often found in the immediate vicinity of each other.

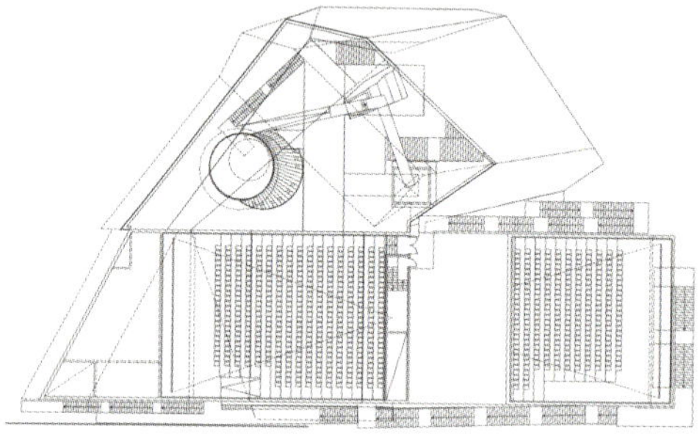

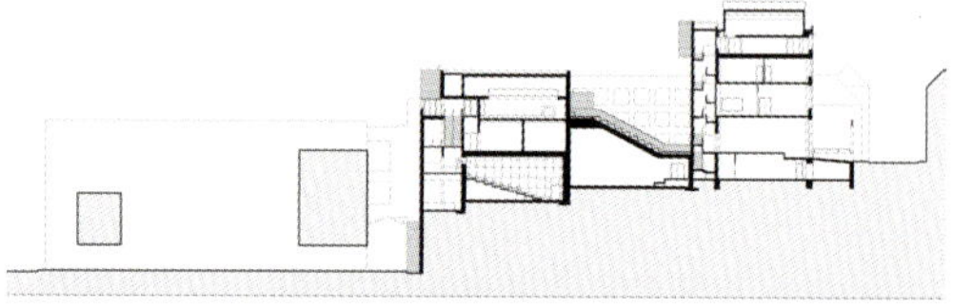

↑↑↑↑ and ↑↑↑ | **Coop Himmelb(l)au with ATP,** UFA-Palast, Dresden, 1998: Urban eye-catcher
↑↑ | **Neutelings Riedijk Architecten,** Artcenter Stuk, Leuven, 2002: Open-air cinema in cultural context
↑ | **De architecten Cie.,** Pathé ArenA, Amsterdam, 2000: Large stairway in large structure
↗ | **Zaha Hadid,** Regium Waterfront, Calabria: Museum of the Mediterranean with cinema
→ | **Coop Himmelb(l)au,** Busan Cinema Center, Busan, South-Korea: Multifunctional and urban

Fixed-focus

Sergei Tchoban Architekt
BDA, nps tchoban voss,
A. M. Prasch S. Tchoban
E. Voss

↑ | **Main audience**
→ | **Lobby,** first floor

Multiplex Cinema Cubix

Berlin

The multiplex cinema with 2,400 seats demanded a reinterpretation of the inner-city cinema theme with an extraordinary spatial concept. On a 37 by 46 meter plot, a cinema on four levels hovers over the square. The strict, compact theater order is dictated by the minimal available area and creates clear communication and urban views from the lobby, which offers scenes of Alexanderplatz environs. Similarly to the rotated orientation of the nine screens on four levels, the façade communicates the impression of an outer skin in horizontal motion. Glass panes overlap on corners and accent the diagonal relationships of the interior and the exterior, whereby glass foyer bays noticeably project from the otherwise flush façade.

Address: Rathausstraße 1, 10178 Berlin, Germany. **Interior Design:** nps tchoban voss with the collaboration of Karl and Klaus Schwitzke. **Light art:** Julian Rosefeldt. **Light and advertising engineering:** Kersten Neon-technik. **Artwork:** Anett Stuth, Galerie Paula Böttcher, Berlin. **Client:** TLG Immobiliengesellschaft mbH, Berlin/Brandenburg. **Completion:** 2001. **Largest screen diameter:** 25 m. **Sound equipment:** Dolby Digital, DTS. **Kind of projection:** 35 mm projection. **Main materials:** Nero Impala polished. **Setting:** inner city.

↑ | **Façade by night,** television tower in the background

← | **Longitudinal section**

← | **Sketch,** lobby and escalator
↓ | **View by night**

DTA Architects / Dermot Reynolds, Colin Mackay

↑ | **Screen** in red color coding
→ | **Screen** with alternative colored acoustic panels

Light House Cinema

Smithfield

In refurbishing the Light House Cinema located within the Smithfield Market, the architects took care to integrate a variety of screen sizes to ensure a diverse cinematic program and to be able to extend runs of popular films for longer periods. The architectural challenge of this project was to combine the insertion of four cinema volumes into existing basement voids while creating an informal circulation route. Each of the four volumes has a consistent color coding which expresses the thematic diversity in accordance to the spatial structure and size of the rooms. Walls, furniture and floors were designed to optimize the cinematic experience while maintaining a unique character.

PROJECT FACTS

Address: Blackhall Walk, Smithfield 7, Dublin, Ireland. **Client:** Light House Cinema Ltd., Fusano Properties. **Completion:** 2008. **Number of seats:** all audiences: 620; main audience: 279. **Largest screen diameter:** 14.12 m. **Sound equipment:** JBL. **Kind of projection:** 35 mm, future proofed for digital projection. **Additional functions:** cafeteria, exhibition space, informal projection spaces. **Main materials:** aluminum, fabric (seating and accoustic panels cladding). **Setting:** inner city.

↑ | **Interior view,** seating area
← | **Stairs and elevator**

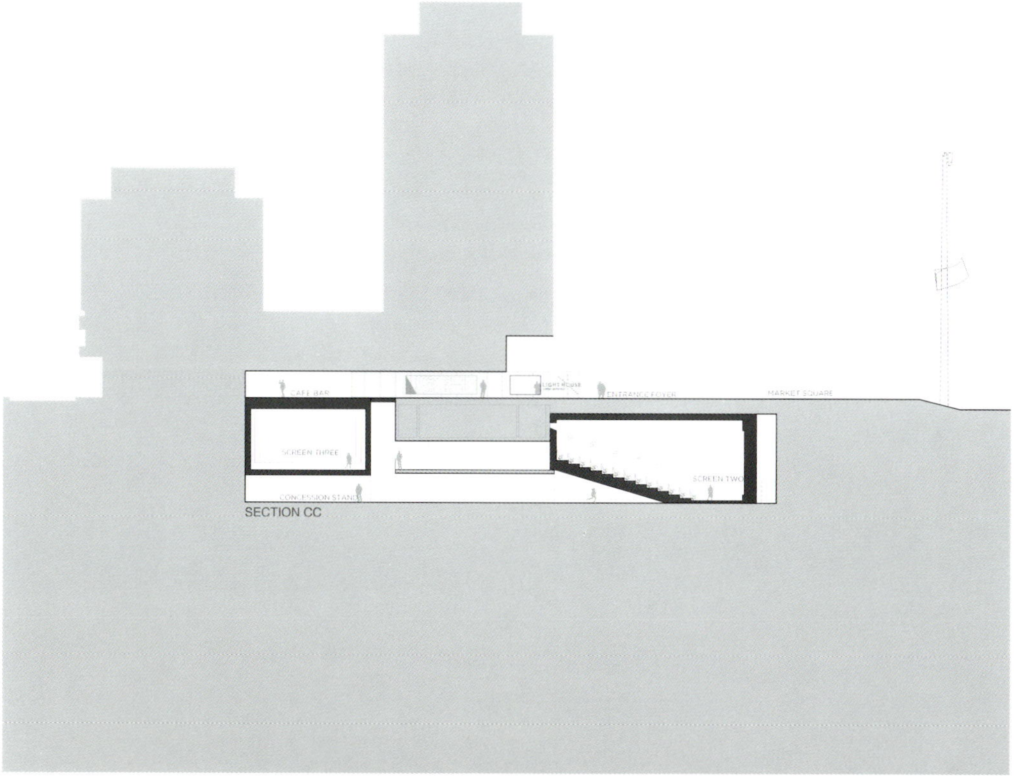

← | **Section**
↓ | **Screen** with alternative colored seating furniture

Atelier Christian de Portzamparc

↑ | Perspective
→ | Cinema and Champs-Libres-building

Pathé Gaumont

Rennes

The project is situated in Rennes, close to the new train station and Champs Libres, another project inaugurated by Christian de Portzamparc in 2006. The multiplex of 13 theater rooms is part of the general organization of the esplanade Charles de Gaulle (urban master plan by Nicolas Michelin). The project is structured by a transversal grand hall, which leads to two floor levels. The hall was designed to give shape to one of the front façades on this esplanade. Its architecture consists of large horizontal planes and slanting lines on which the daylight reflects. The shades of the artificial lights at night create a dialogue with Champs-Libres, further emphasized by the similar materials and volumes of the newly constructed building. The concrete was developed in a special way with architectonic moulds designed by Christian de Portzamparc and the sculptor Martin Wallace.

PROJECT FACTS

Address: Corner of Alliés Court and Magenta Boulevard, 35000 Rennes, France. **Client:** Europalaces (Pathé-Gaumont). **Completion:** 2008. **Number of seats:** all audiences: 2.800; main audience: 443. **Largest screen diameter:** 17.1 m. **Sound equipment:** Cinemeccanica. **Additional functions:** restaurant, multimedia bookshop, literary café. **Main materials:** concrete (developed with architectonic moulds designed by Christian de Portzamparc and the sculptor Martin Wallace), glass, aluminum. **Setting:** urban.

↑ | Front
← | Mezzanin plan
↙ | Ground floor plan

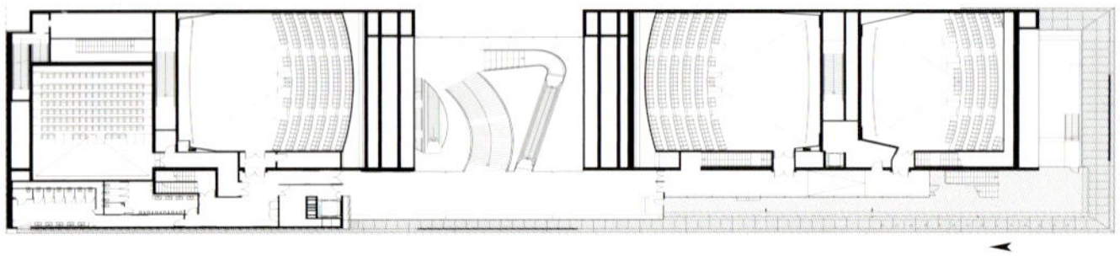

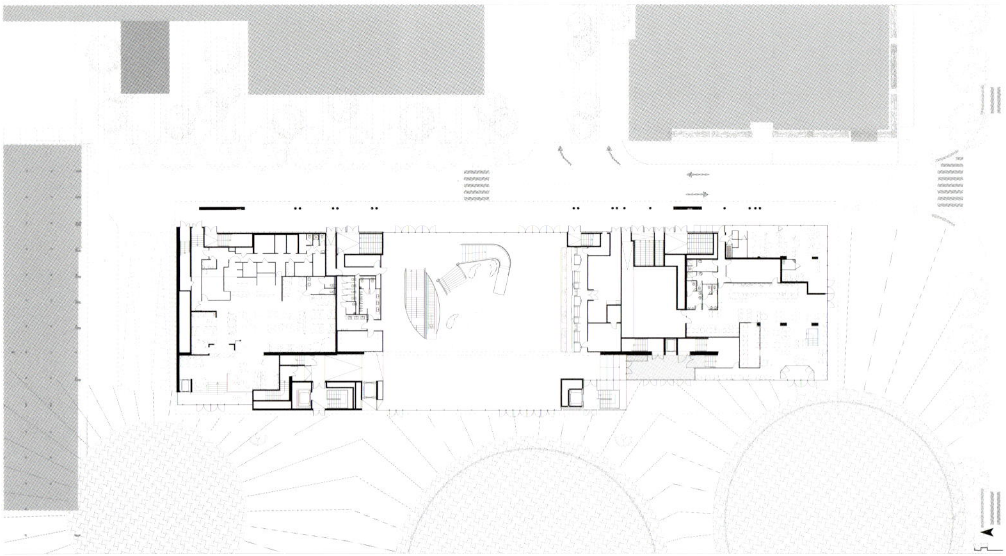

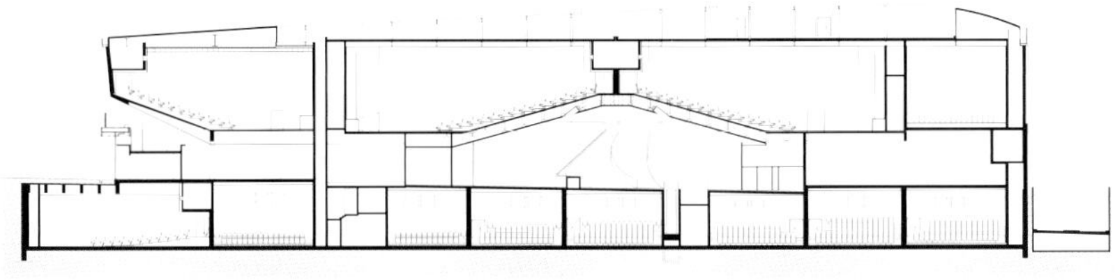

← | Section
↓ | Cinema in dialogue with Champs-Libres-building

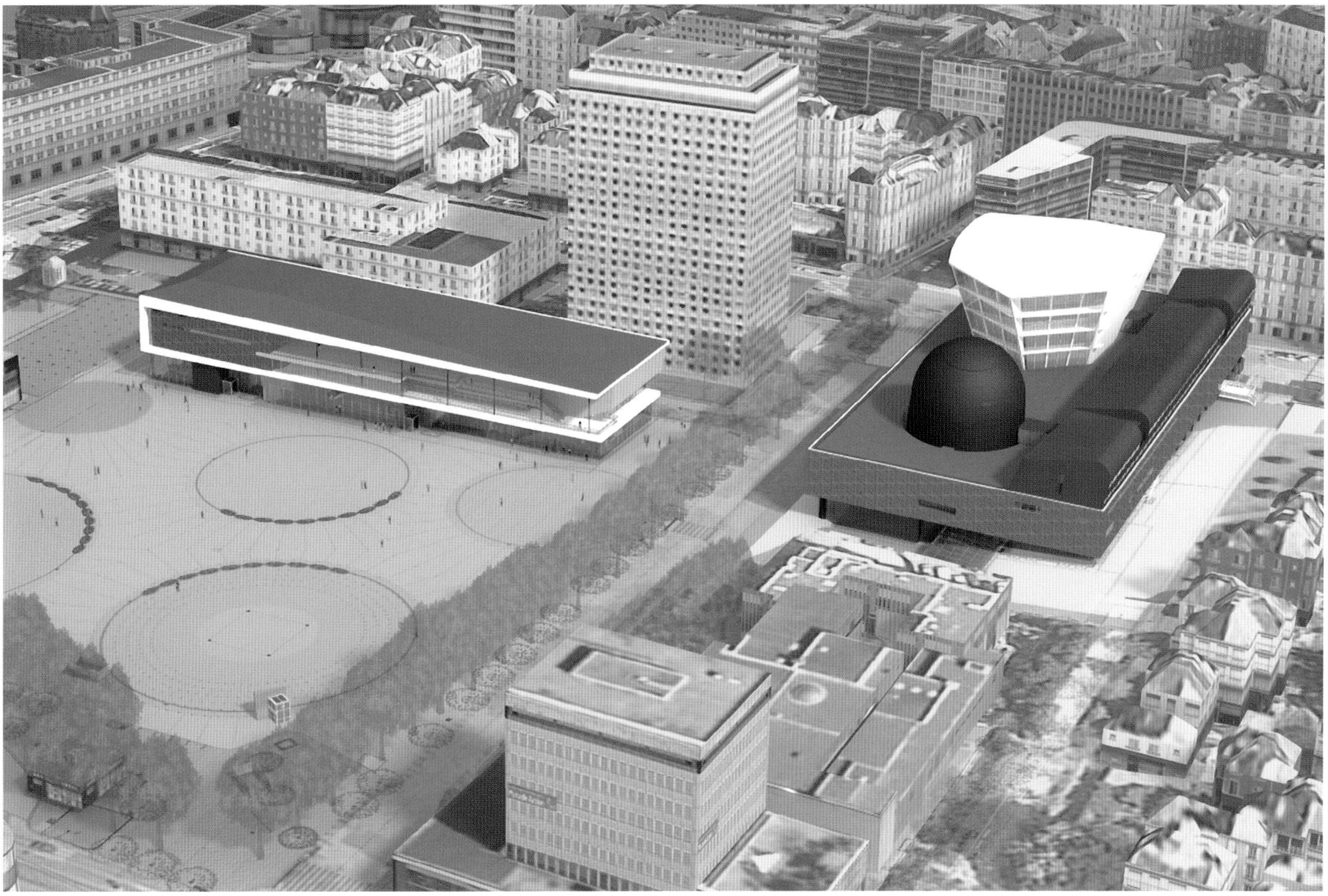

↑ | **AFI expansion** with embedded logo
→ | **Restored** original theater entry façade

AFI Silver Theater

Silver Spring

The cinema was designed in 1938 by the architect John Eberson and features a highly articulated art deco motif of sweeping curvilinear forms married with ornate fabric wall murals. To restore the theater, Gensler's team went back to the archive, unearthing photos and news clippings covering the Silver Theater's first grand opening. They also salvaged scraps of fabric from the original wall coverings and carpets to recreate the theater's rich color palette. The restored building is combined with an expansion which gives AFI two more high-tech theaters, exhibit spaces, a cafe, and offices. The theaters may also function as modern broadcast studios. At the recent grand opening, Clint Eastwood pronounced the theater "a work of art".

PROJECT FACTS

Address: 8619 Colesville Road, Silver Spring, MD 20910, USA. **Participants in planning:** American Film Institute, Montgomery County. **Client:** American Film Institute. **Completion:** 2003. **Number of seats:** 675. **Largest screen diameter:** 12,84 m. **Sound equipment:** THX-standard. **Kind of projection:** 16 mm, 35 mm, 70 mm vertical, digital beam. **Additional functions:** cultural center, meeting rooms, AFI offices. **Main materials:** exterior: curtainwall, brick, stucco; interior: fabric, painted drywall. **Setting:** inner city.

↑ | **Main Auditorium** with movable proscenium
← | **New center** lobby with cinema exhibit space

← | Restored original theater
↙ | Ground floor plan

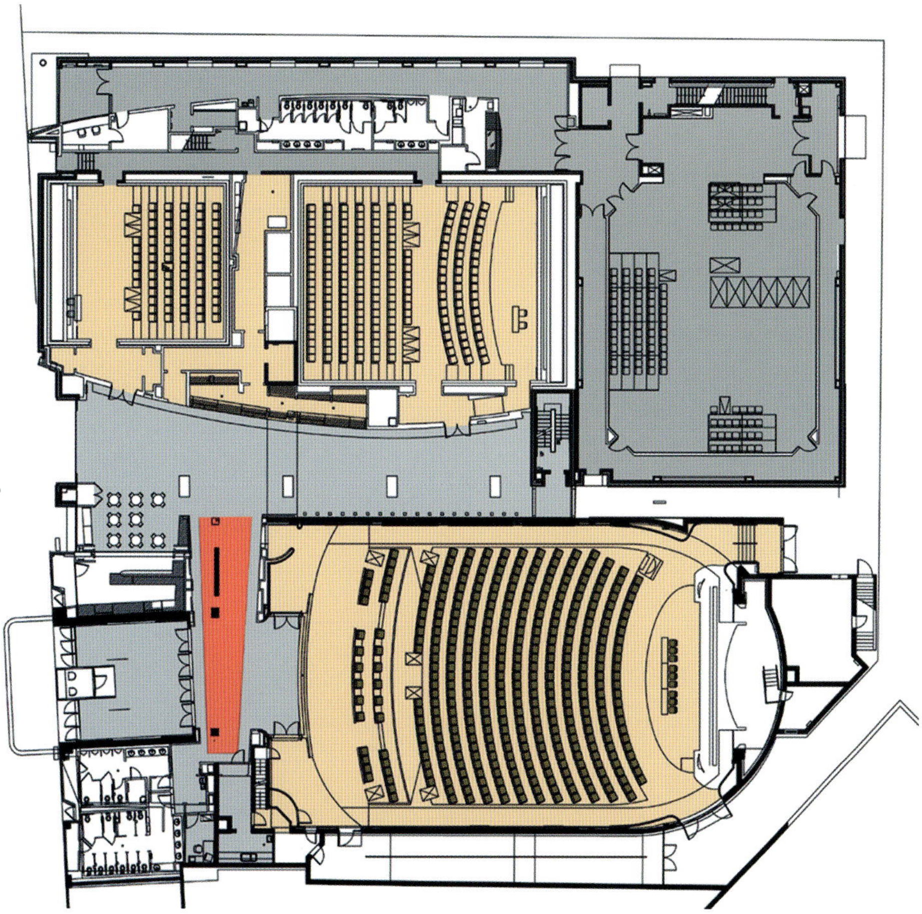

BURO II /
Hendrik Vermoortel (CEO),
Tom Vandorpe (project director)

↑ | **Entrance area**
→ | **View of façade** and roof structure

Kinepolis Ostend

Oostende

In Oostende, the Kinepolis Group took on the challenge of building a new cinema complex close by the city center, near the Royal Galleries at the Thermae Palace Hotel and racecourse. Their goal was not only to produce a good integration in both the urban and landscape surroundings, but also to achieve an important upgrade of the whole area by creating a functional, attractive and, first and foremost, affordable building. The complex research process started by facing the challenges posed by the landscape: a sloping plot, a 'city dune', an extensive transformation that would hide elements located below ground. At the end, the choice was made to create a subtle, but rationally designed building which is partially sunk.

PROJECT FACTS

Address: Koningin Astridlaan 12, 8400 Oostende, Belgium. **Planning partner:** Ro Berteloot architects. **Client:** Kinepolis Group. **Completion:** 2007. **Sound equipment:** Dolby Digital. **Kind of projection:** digital, 3D. **Main materials:** zinc. **Setting:** inner city.

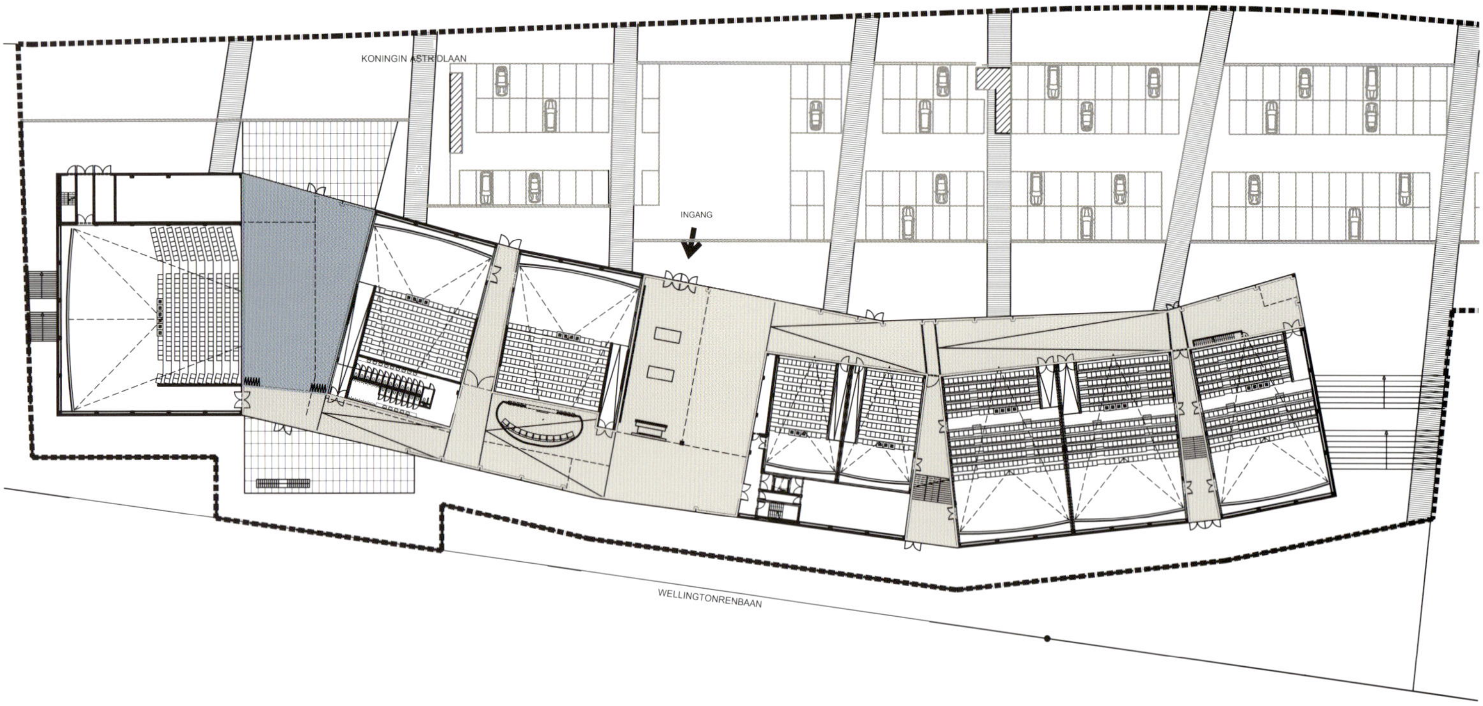

↑ | **Ground floor plan**
← | **Detail,** façade cladding

← | **Parking area and front façade**
↓ | **Parking area and front façade**, different angle

Franklin Azzi Architecture

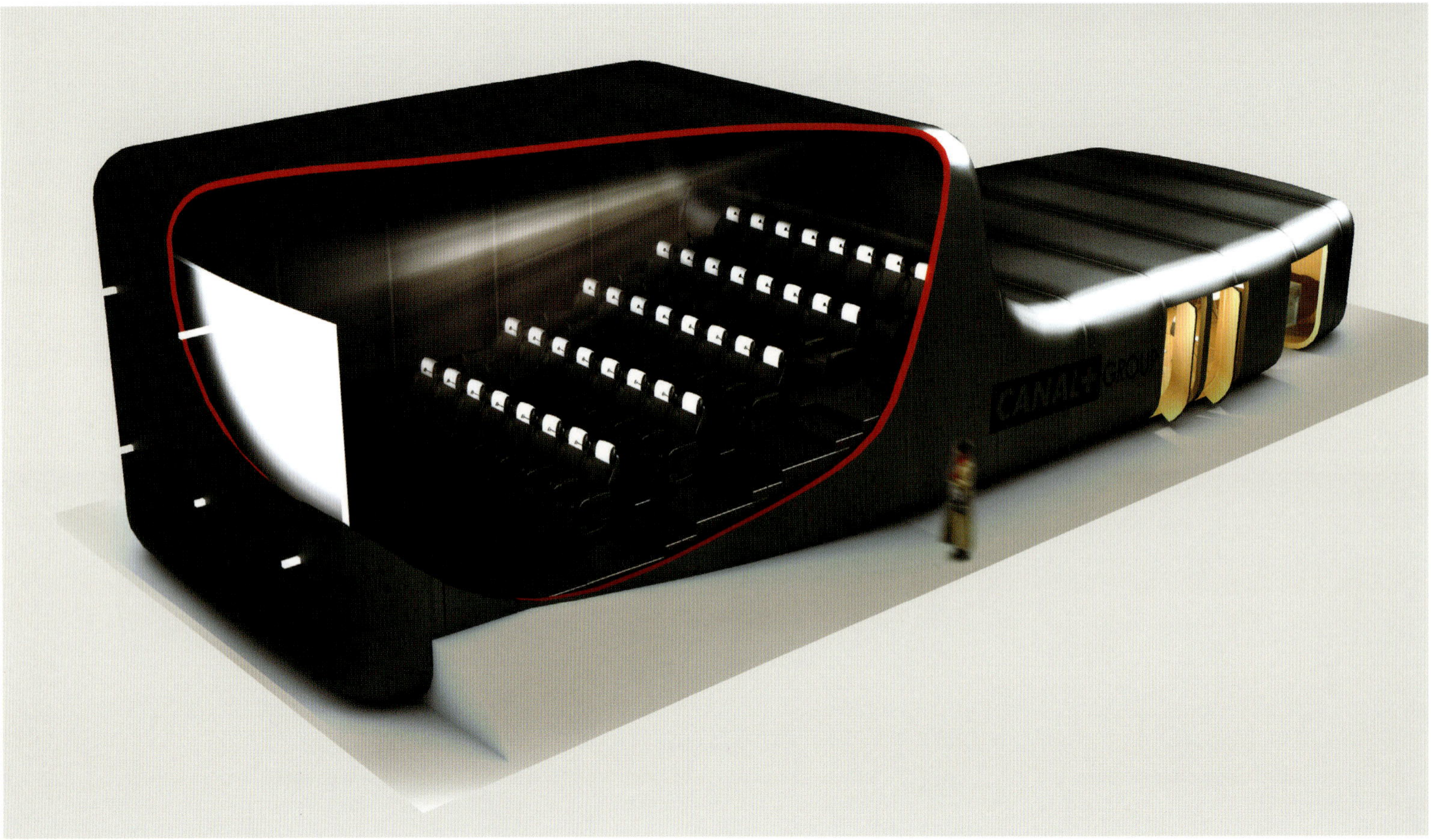

↑ | **Cinema body and interior**

Canal+

Issy les Moulineaux

The main challenge in designing the Canal+ building was to insert new functions into an existing building shell according to the principle of Russian matryoshka dolls. The designers decided to create envelopes housing different functions which include a hall, a cinema and a VIP lounge. A monolithic body with a seemingly smooth and reflective surface forms the skin of the movie theater communicating the special character of its interior to visitors. A modular approach was chosen for the cinema's interior. The seats are hinged on rails which may be raised and lowered to adjust to the needs of different events.

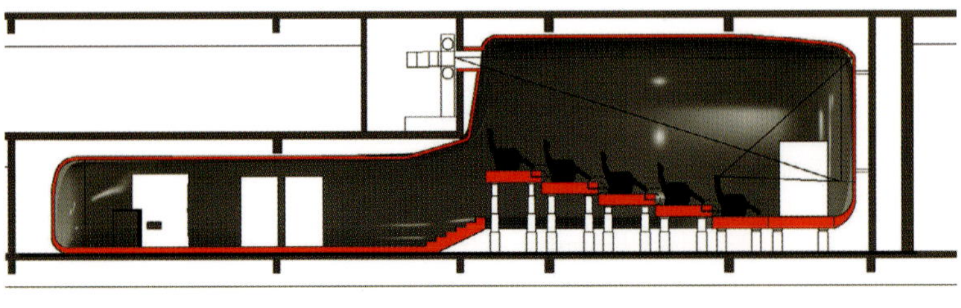

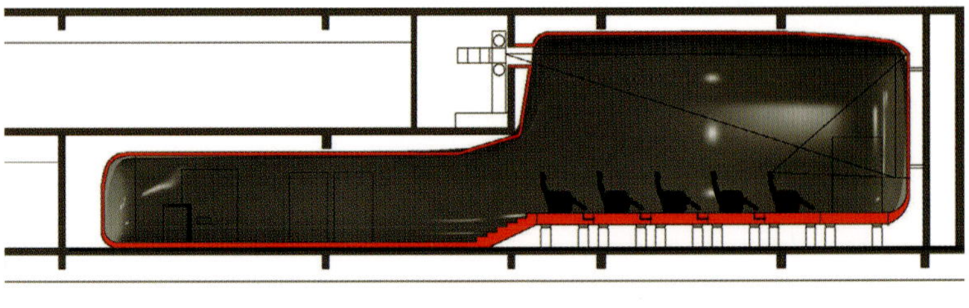

PROJECT FACTS

Address: 1 place du spectacle, 92863 Issy les Moulineaux, France. **Client:** Canal+ Group. **Completion:** 2010. **Additional functions:** VIP lounge, reception. **Main materials:** glass, steel, black leather. **Setting:** urban.

↑ | **Interior view,** hall and reception

↙ | **Plans,** showing modularity

↓ | **Cinema body and interior,** monolithic countenance

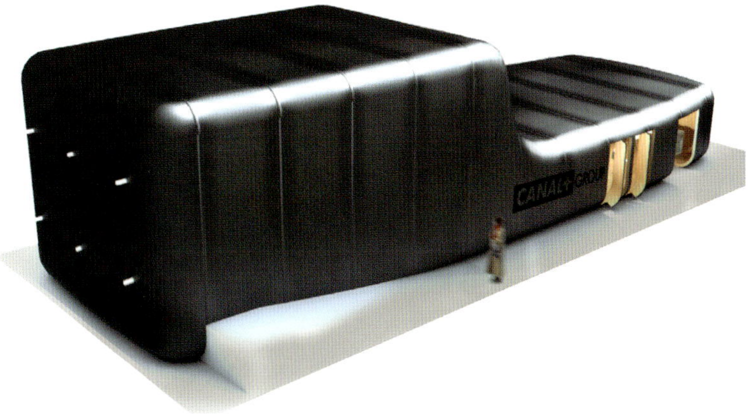

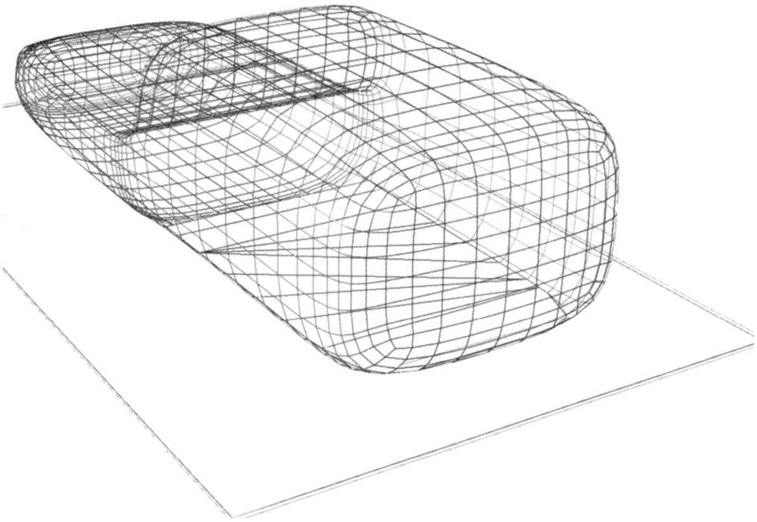

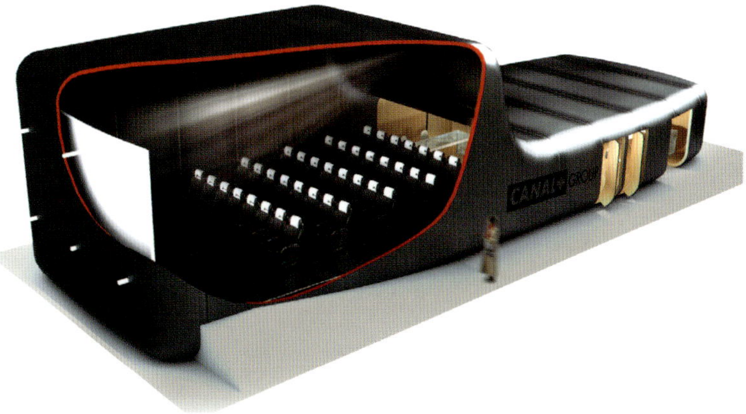

↑ | **East elevation** by night
↗ | **Side elevation** by night
→ | **Staircase,** first floor area

Expansion of Program Cinema

Dresden

The original 'east' program cinema building in Dresden has been expanded in order to increase schedule variety. By tearing down perimeter houses facing the street, space was created for a three-story building to accommodate four new theaters with a range of seating options. The cinemas are connected via a large foyer, which in turn flows into the existing foyer. The sculptural stairs let the levels be physically experienced. The protruding foyer building with a two-story glass façade framed by fair faced concrete forms the building's image from the street. The cinema building has a window front which stretches along the length of the street, offering ample space for presenting posters.

PROJECT FACTS

Address: Schandauer Straße 73, 01277 Dresden, Germany. **Client:** Programmkino Ost GmbH. **Completion:** 2009. **Number of seats:** all audiences: 571, main audience: 204. **Largest screen diameter:** approx. 10 m. **Sound equipment:** Dolby Digital 7.1, Kinoton FP30 hearing impaired loop. **Main materials:** exterior: fairfaced concrete, corrugated iron, interior: stucco, magnesium floor. **Setting:** urban.

←←| **Foyer,** ground floor area with bar and food counter
← | **Interior view,** bar in red
↓ | **Section,** cinema structure

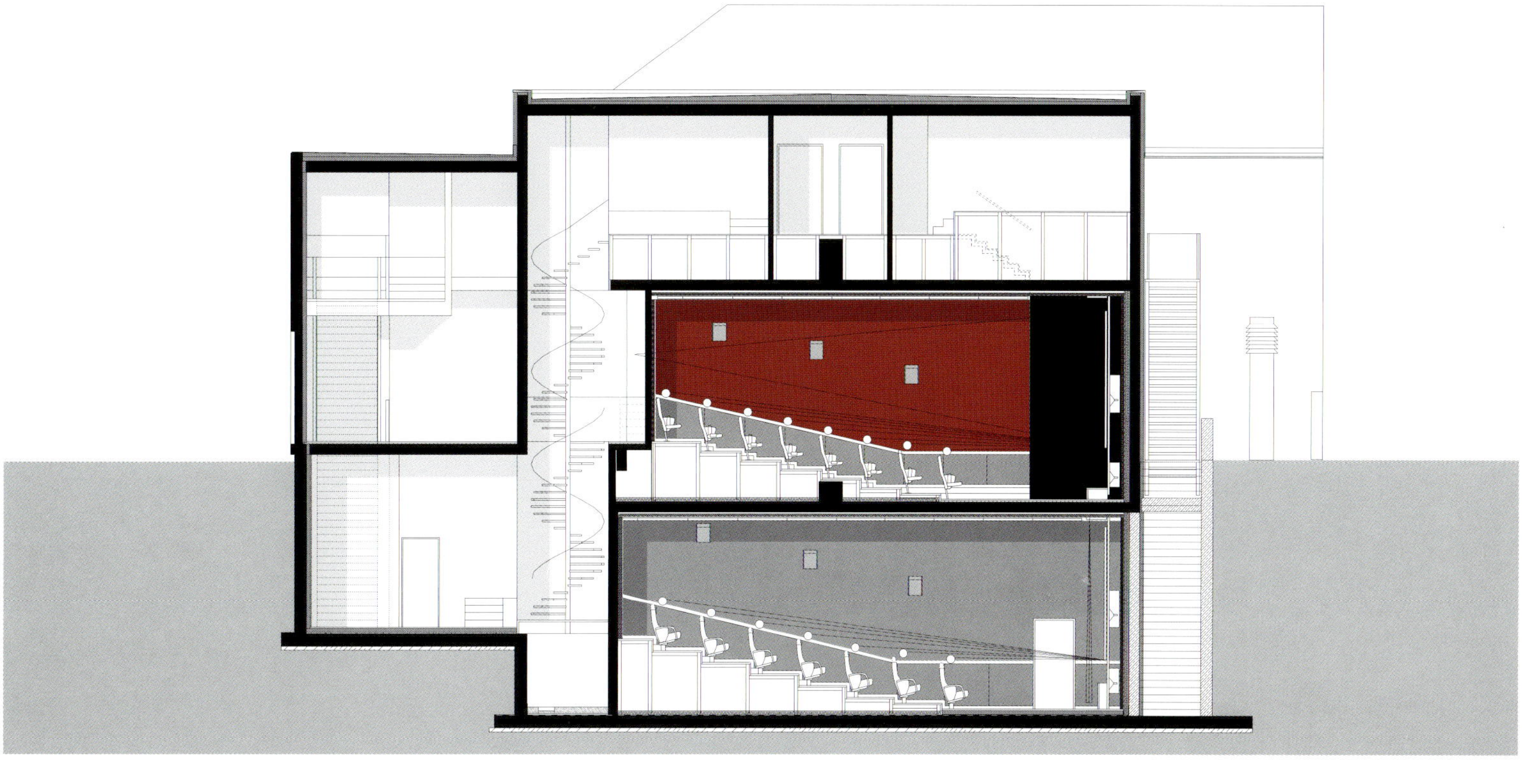

↑ | **General view,** street side
→ | **Staircase** to the lounge

Filmburg Kronach

Kronach

The Filmburg Kronach theater has undergone a modernization and has been expanded by two cinemas via the addition of multiple structural sections. The first section stands apart from the original building thanks to its form and choice of materials, reiterating that the whole building occupies the function of "Entertainment". Additionally, the idea of visualizing the temporal dimension of the medium of cinema influenced the design of the interior décor, form and façade. A new cinema and an expanded entrance area with a bistro were created as a result. In the second section, the existing old building has been transformed into a modern cinema complex. The old theater has been divided into two independent movie theaters. Here, the quality of the interior design is what matters: acoustic insulation, the steepest possible stepwise incline, new cinema chairs and modern projection technology step into focus.

PROJECT FACTS

Address: Schwedenstraße 37, 96317 Kronach, Germany. **Client:** Filmburg Kronach GbR. **Completion:** 2005. **Number of seats:** all audiences: 399; main audience: 147. **Additional functions:** gastronomy, apartment, beer garden. **Main materials:** exterior: titanium zinc; interior: stucco. **Setting:** urban.

↑ | **Audience 01**
← | **Sections**

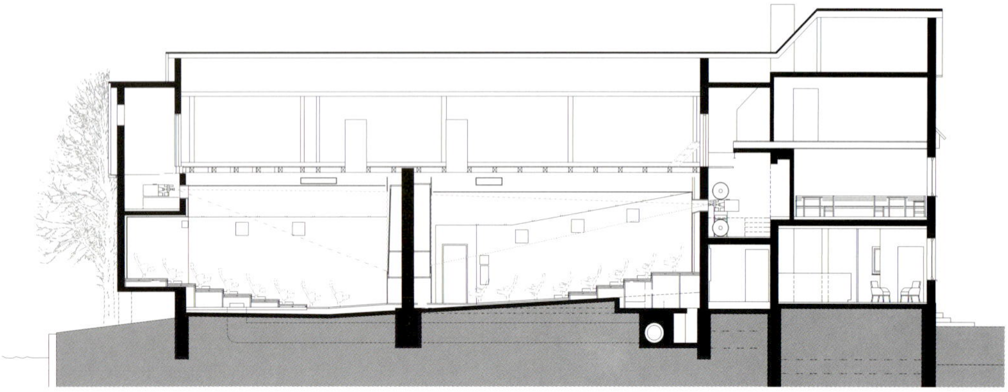

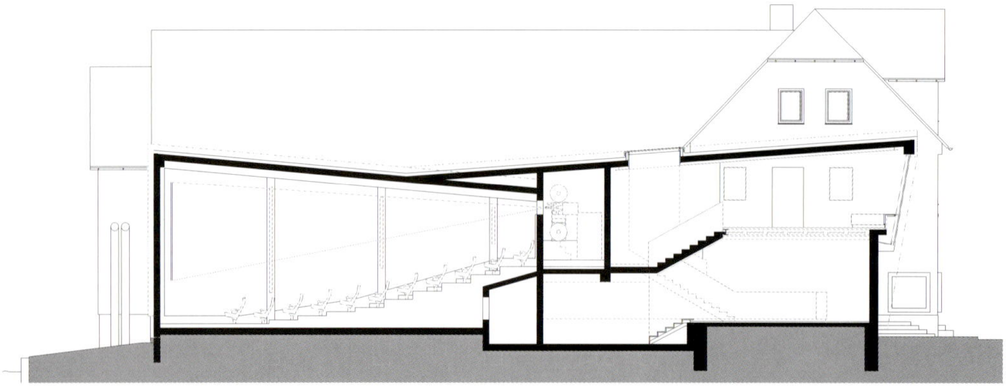

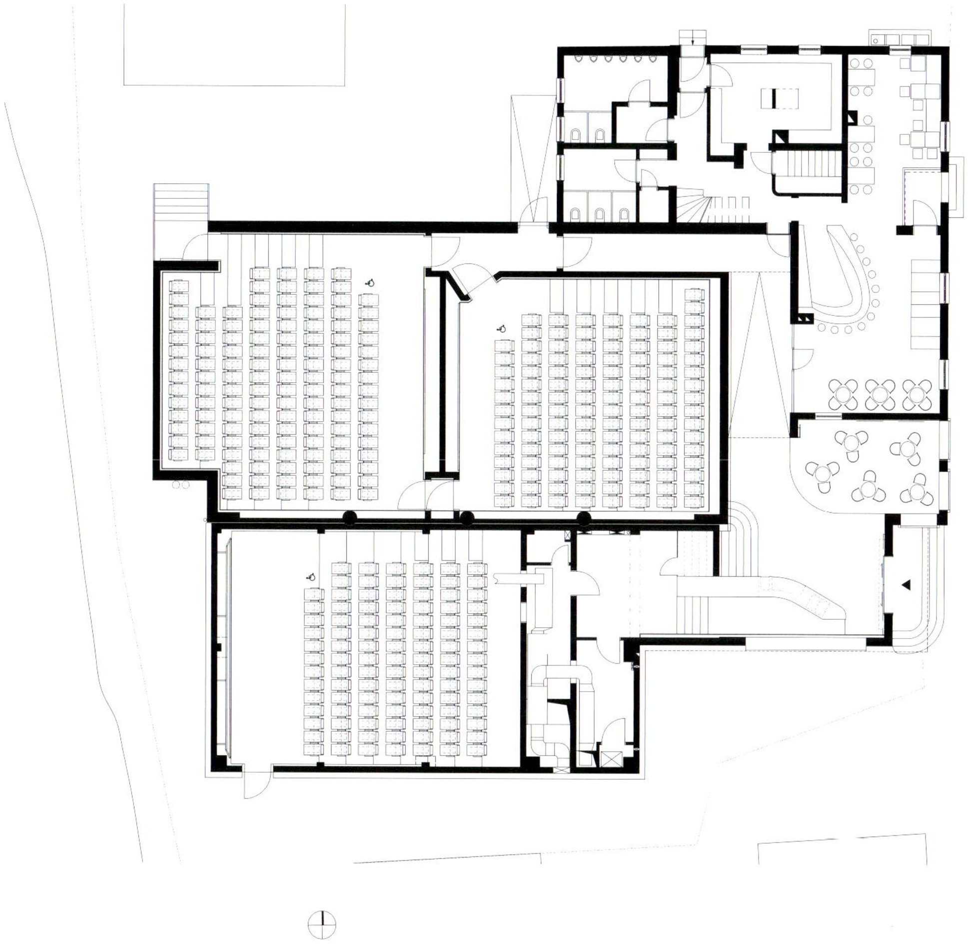

← | **Ground floor plan**
↓ | **Front elevation**, audience 03

↑ | **View by night,** from river Danube
↗ | **Entrance area,** bar and cashpoint
→ | **Staircase**

Cinema Wöhrden West

Tuttlingen

Located in Tuttlingen near the shore of the Danube river, the "Wöhrden West" district was restructured as part of an urban development measure. In addition to a multiplex cinema with 833 seats in five theaters and dining facilities, three further buildings were created. The current urban planning concept of the Wöhrdenkopf is dominated by the cinema and administration hub. The cinema building design is based on light and shadow as an art form. The theaters are visibly stacked on top of each other and accessible via stairs and ramps from the Danube side. The exterior cover consists of glass façades with a suspended metal mesh that presents clear vision to the outside and the inside.

PROJECT FACTS

Address: In Wöhrden, 78532 Tuttlingen, Germany. **Client:** Tuttlinger Wohnbau. **Completion:** 2004. **Number of seats:** all audiences: 833, main audience: 229. **Largest screen diameter:** 12.36 m. **Additional functions:** gastronomy, offices, residences, practices. **Main materials:** exterior: glass, aluminum, stucco; interior: fairfaced concrete. **Setting:** inner city.

↑ | Intermediate level

← | Site plan

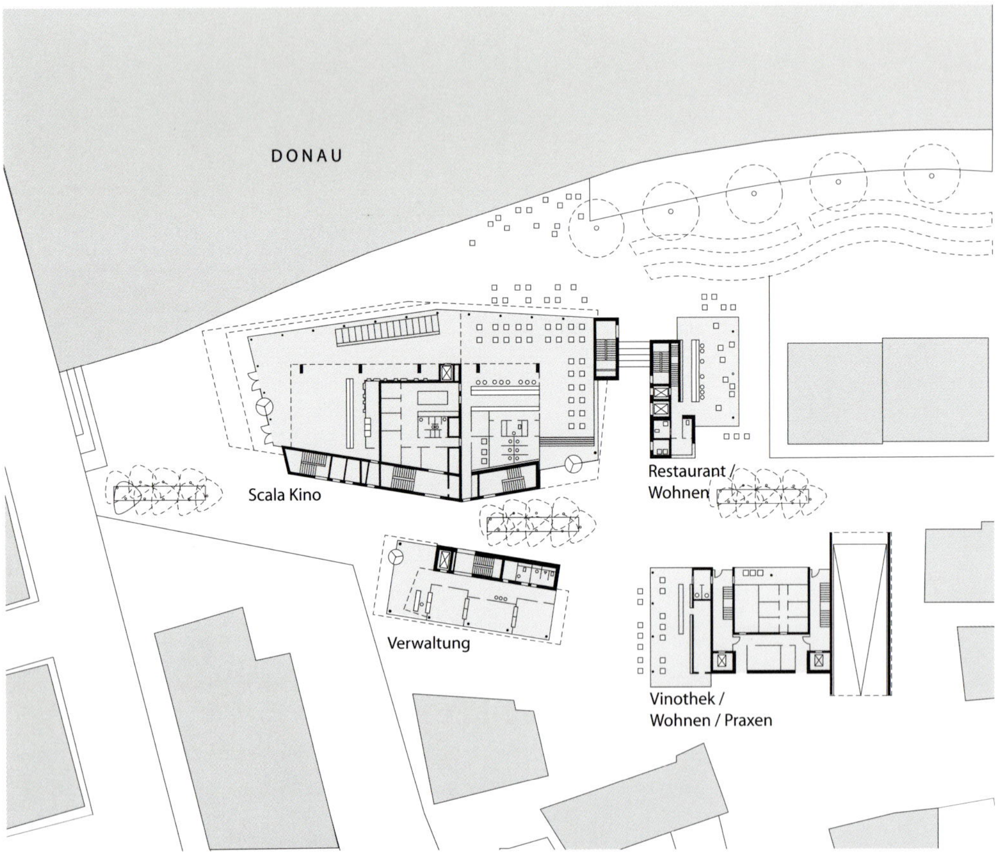

← | Stairs
↓ | Ramp

James Law Cybertecture International

↑ | **Audience,** each theater has been upholstered with sumptuous French leather seats.
→ | **Interior view,** a modern sculpture protruding outwards to issue tickets

AMC Pacific Place

Hong Kong

James Law made this cinema a programmatic building for his Cybertecture. He fuses luxury and astute technology in state-of-the-art architecture. For example, the ticketing box is no longer enclosed in a conventional glass box, but is more akin to a modern sculpture or a chic hotel lobby, protruding outwards to skillfully incorporate the ticket dispensing technology. The walls comprise sculptural, organic shapes molded together to form a U-shaped corridor; the aerodynamic ceiling has a metallic coating witch carries a river-like pattern throughout the foyer of the cinema. The cinema's design has been configured so that from the moment patrons arrive, they are transported to a totally new experience.

PROJECT FACTS

Address: Pacific Place, 88 Queensway Road, Hong Kong, China. **Client:** AMC Cinema. **Completion:** 2006. **Number of seats:** all audiences: 600, VIP audience: 39. **Largest screen diameter:** 6.71 m. **Sound equipment:** SRD-EX audio system. **Additional functions:** restaurants, Aqua bar, refreshment bar. **Main materials:** metallic coating carries, stainless steel, leather. **Setting:** urban.

↑ | **Foyer** with food counters

← | **Floor plan**

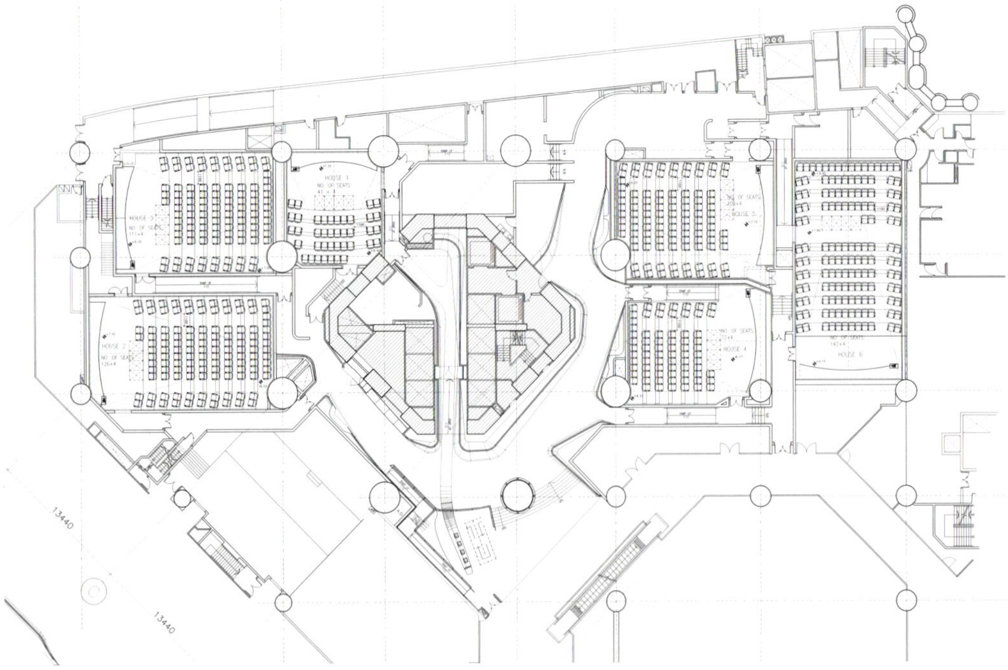

← | **Lobby,** the entrance of AMC Cinema

↓ | **Corridor**

Freyrie & Pestalozza
Architetti Associatti

↑ | **Façade** with main entrance and parking area

UCI Cinemas

Curno

This cinema, which is the first UCI multiplex cinema in Italy, is divided into nine theaters, providing room for a total of 2,500 visitors. The foyer, ticket office and a café are located on the ground level. The upper floor houses the theaters, a restaurant and technical facilities. An organic system of vertical and horizontal connections allows an orderly organization of visitor movement. The theaters are the result of a careful ergonometric study which took particular consideration of the optical system and seating comfort. The interior design is a play of light and color which uses indirect and direct lighting and different surface structures and materials to complete the overall impression of the building.

PROJECT FACTS

Address: Curno, BG, Italy. **Planning partners:** J&A Consultants (project manager), Cole Jarman (sound), Milanoprogetti (landscaping). **Client:** UCI. **Completion:** 1999. **Number of seats:** all audiences: 2,500, main audience: 452. **Sound equipment:** Dolby. **Kind of projection:** widescreen, cinemascope. **Main materials:** exterior: concrete panels, interior: fabric, carpet, gypsum. **Setting:** suburban.

↑ | **Interior view,** foyer
↙ | **Plan**

↑ | **Interior view,** escalator
↓ | **Interior view,** stairs

Studio Ramin Visch

↑ | **Staircase,** view from upper floor
→ | **Cafè and wooden structure,** as envelope for the cinema auditoria

Cinema Het Ketelhuis

Amsterdam

A free-standing, bulky structure rises through the interior of a converted boiler house on the site of the former Westergasfabriek gas works in Amsterdam. The inner volume contains two 50-seat film auditoria at ground-floor level with a larger, 143-seat auditorium above them. The connection between these two levels is provided by a suspended steel staircase which climbs on the outside of the volume. Apart from the first landing, which receives additional support from a tension rod, the staircase is secured only by mountings at the top and bottom. The strips of wood visible from the outside are of larch, and form a cladding which smoothly envelopes the bulging form of this huge piece of furniture, wrapping around the three auditoria to form a compact volume.

PROJECT FACTS

Address: Pazzanistraat 4, 1014 DB Amsterdam, The Netherlands. **Client:** Foundation Het Ketelhuis. **Completion:** 2006. **Number of seats:** all audiences: 500; main audience: 143. **Largest screen diameter:** 8 m. **Sound equipment:** Dolby Digital 7.1. **Kind of projection:** 35 mm/video beamer. **Additional functions:** café. **Main materials:** wood, carpet. **Setting:** urban.

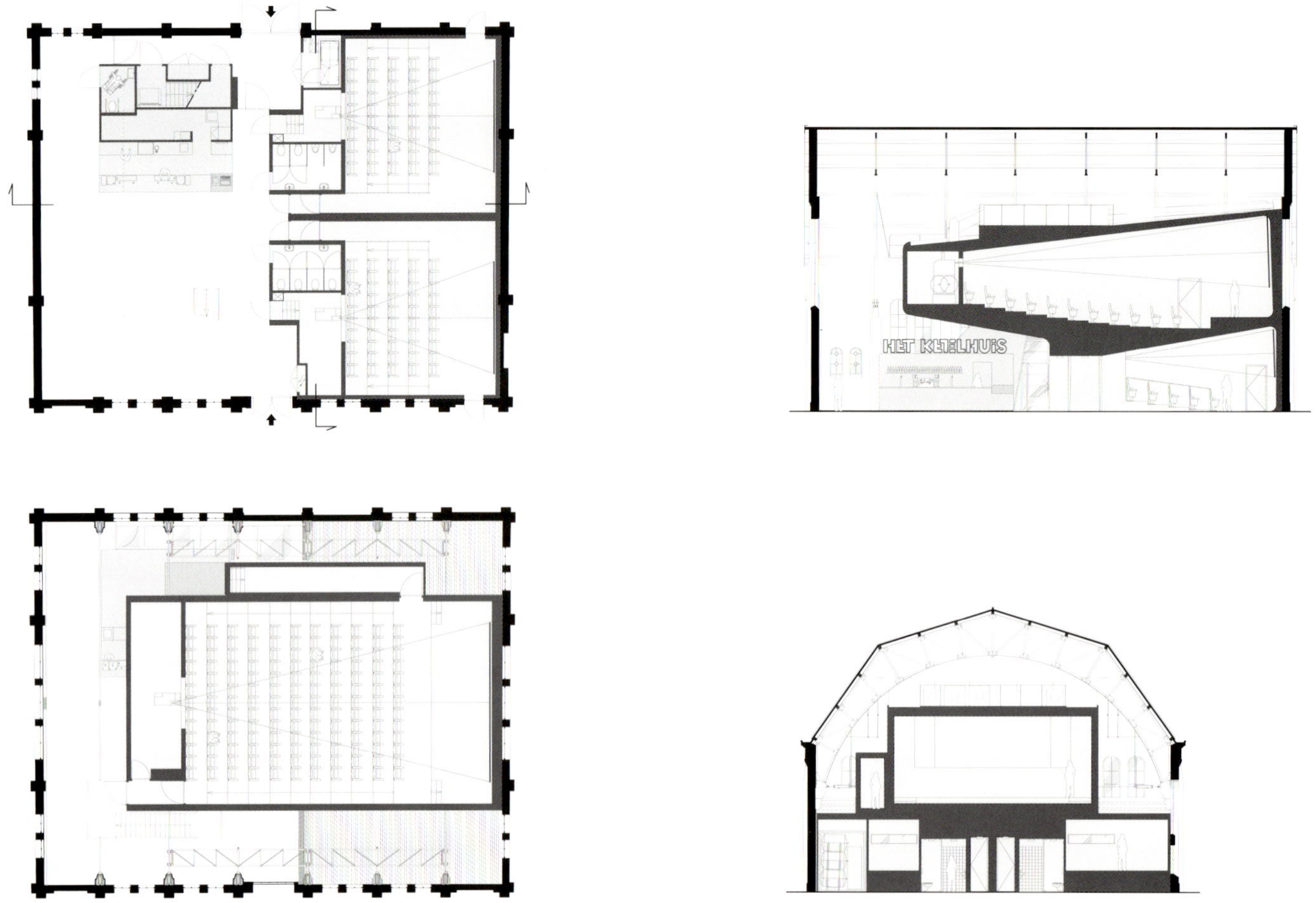

↑ | **Plans and elevations**

← | **Entrance to auditorium 1,** view from staircase

←↓ | View inside different auditoria

DP6 architectuurstudio

↑ | **Street side façade** with pond and colorful illumination

→ | **Total view** in direction of city center

Utopolis

Emmen

The town of Emmen lies surrounded by a flat agricultural landscape. Visitors entering the town from the southwest find themselves abruptly within the town center, experiencing virtually no transition. A new multiplex cinema is constructed at this location to act as an entrance to the town. Leaving the N364 speedway, motorists approach the building from its most dramatic angle, with the movie theater's sloping underside floating above an expanse of water. Seven theaters with a total of 1,250 seats, as well as a café and a bar are part of this cinema complex. The theaters are spacious and steeply sloped to provide optimum viewing conditions. To allow all projection rooms to be located on one level, the theaters have been arranged in a single row.

PROJECT FACTS

Address: Westeind 70, 7811 ME Emmen, The Netherlands. **Planning partners:** Stubeco (structural planning), DGMR Raadgevende Ingenieurs (building physics), ABT Adviesbureau voor bouwtechniek (construction). **Client:** Utopia Group. **Completion:** 2005. **Number of seats:** 1,290. **Main materials:** steel, stucco, glass. **Setting:** urban.

↑ | **Interior view,** glass façade and approach to theaters
← | **Site plan**
→ | **Façade detail**

Robert Majkut Design

↑ | **View of counter**
↗ | **Detail,** counter decoration
→ | **Seating area**

Multikino Galaxy Centre

Szczecin

Multikino Galaxy Centre communicates a slightly eccentric impression to viewers and visitors alike, even before they step inside. Among the most striking design elements are the semicircular cash boxes dispersed throughout the foyer. The basic idea behind the design of the main hall was to present the cinema as a part of the universal "world of film", where the viewer can not only watch a movie or enjoy interesting interiors, but also feel part of the film universe, vibrant with activity. The Galaxy Centre demonstrates that the glamour and magic of the film industry may be experienced not just in places like Los Angeles, London or New York, but also right here in Szczecin.

PROJECT FACTS

Address: Galaxy Centre, Al. Wyzwolenia 18–20, 70-554 Szczecin, Poland. **Client:** GRUPA ITI. **Completion:** 2007. **Number of seats:** all audiences: 2,165; main audience: 498. **Setting:** inner city.

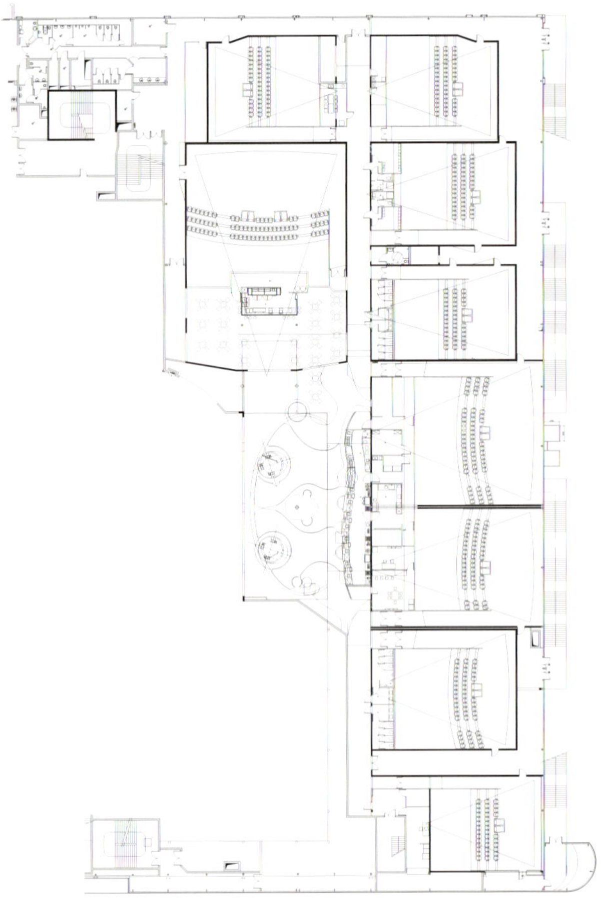

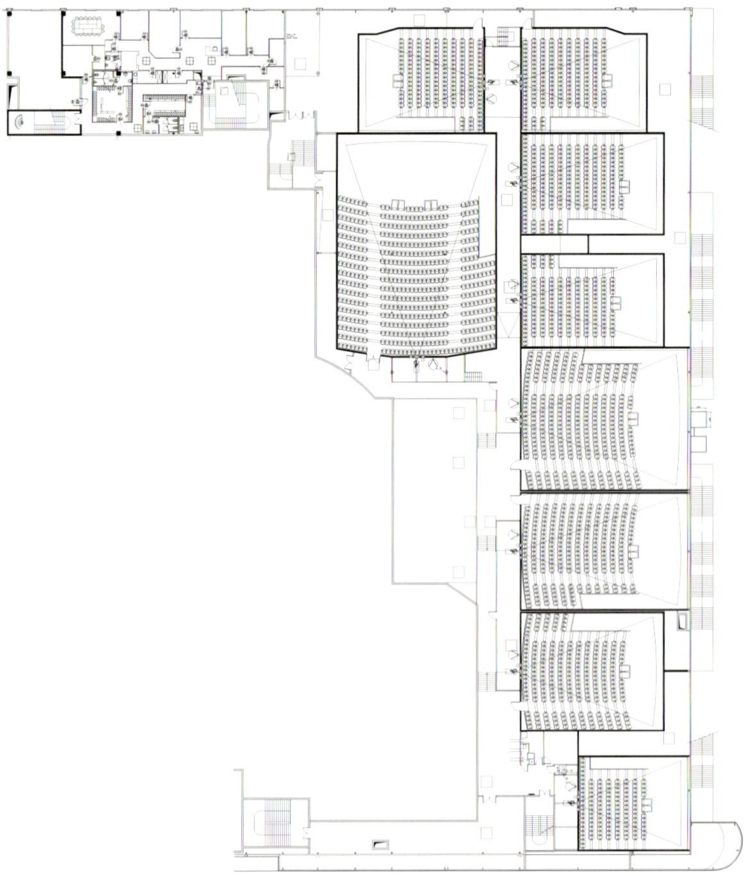

↑ | **Floor plans,** first floor and second floor
← | **View into the hall,** half-round cash boxes and seating furniture

← | **View along the corridor** with entrances to the screens
↓ | **Detail of cash box**

↑ | **Exterior,** along the old part to the annex
→ | **Couch movie theater**

Cinema and Bar Xenix

Zurich

The Xenix cinema is housed in a century-old school pavilion which has been expanded by one-third with an addition. The building's form is unified through the use of a sculptural roof which embraces both the original structure and the addition. Inside, an exciting coming together of the old and the new takes place in the bar area, which is clearly positioned on the interface between the original structure and the extension. By incorporating original atmospheric details, the extension orients itself on the older structure and still manages to create new qualities, such as an entrance façade, which may be completely opened on warm summer nights. The cinema and foyer found in the original building are completely reorganized, whereby the nine couches from the beloved "couch movie theater" have been preserved.

Address: Kanzleistrasse 52, 8004 Zurich, Switzerland. **Architects:** B.Frei and M. Saarinen with Ch. Beerli, L. Pestalozzi, L. Ramakers, S. Stein, D. Winzeler. **Client:** Immobilienbewirtschaftung der Stadt Zürich. **Completion:** 2007. **Original building:** 1904. **Number of seats:** 112. **Largest screen diameter:** 6.09 m. **Sound equipment:** Dolby-Digital 7.1. **Kind of projection:** 35 mm Kinoton FP 20, 16 mm Bauer Selecton, 16 mm Eiki 550 W. **Additional functions:** bar. **Main materials:** wood, aluminum. **Setting:** urban.

↑ | **East façade,** backside
← | **Main façade**

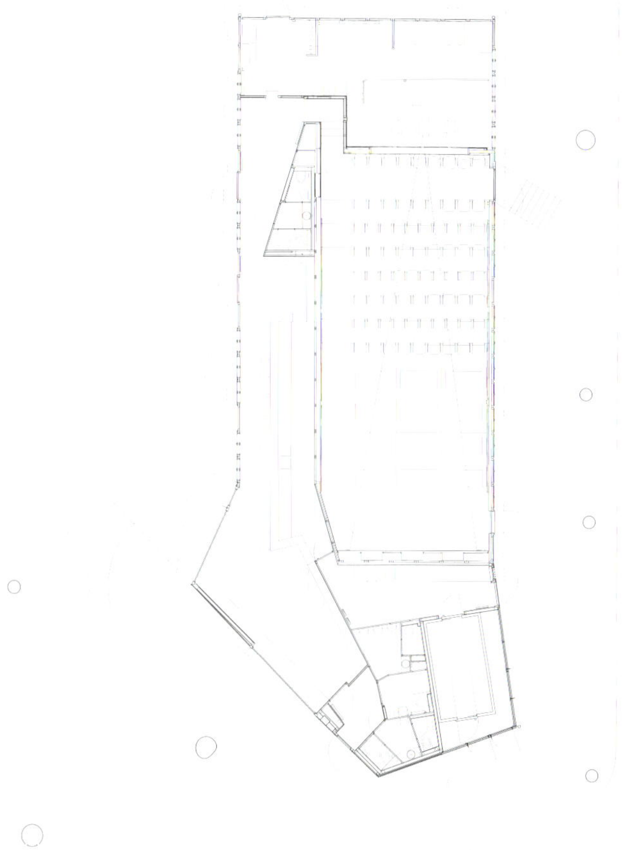

← | Ground floor plan
↓ | Bar

↑ | The screen

BFI IMAX Cinema

London

This 500-seat large-screen IMAX Cinema was built for the British Film Institute and opened in May 1999. At the time of its opening, it was by far the largest screen in Britain, and one of the biggest in the world. The sophistication of the IMAX projection and sound system is matched here by the construction technology. The site is surrounded by traffic, and with the Waterloo and City tube lines just four meters below the surface, the entire upper superstructure had to be set on anti-vibration bearings to prevent the transfer of noise into the auditorium. Not only does the cinema consistently attract the highest attendances for films shown there, but with the flourishing of the surrounding vegetation, it has come to symbolise the regeneration of the entire area.

PROJECT FACTS

Address: 1 Charlie Chaplin Walk, Southbank, Waterloo, London SE1 8XR, United Kingdom. **Planning partners:** Anthony Hunt Associates (structural engineer), Mace Ltd (managing contractor), Northcrofts (quantity surveyor), TME (services engineer), John Medhurst (horticultural). **Artist:** Sir Howard Hodgkin. **Client:** British Film Institute. **Completion:** 1999. **Largest screen diameter:** 34 m. **Sound equipment:** 11,600 watt digital surround sound. **Kind of projection:** IMAX; 35 mm & digital. **Setting:** inner city

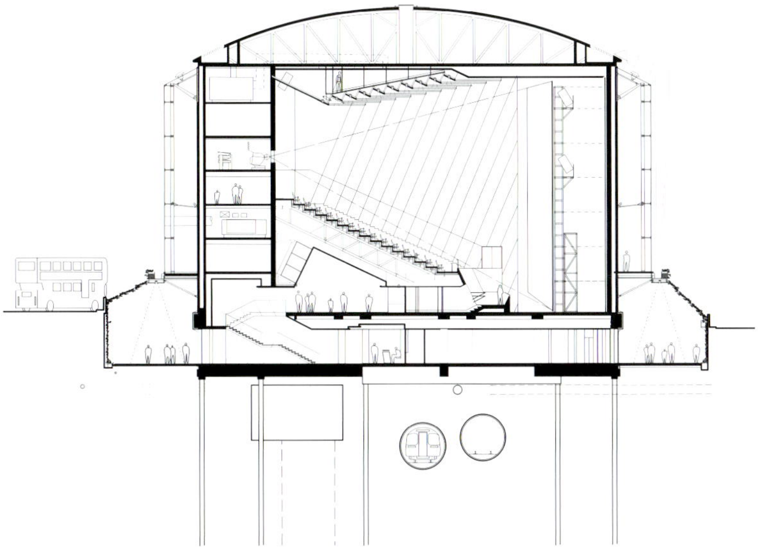

↑ | **Section**
↓ | **Inside the façade**

↑ | **Front elevation**
↓ | **Façade,** structure between wall and glass

↑ | **Electra in use**
→ | **Tyneside** taking its place in the nightlife of Newcastle

Tyneside Cinema

Newcastle upon Tyne

The refurbishment of the historic Tyneside Cinema includes a dazzling roof extension to house two new cinema screens, a new education suite including a film production space, editing suites and digital cinema technology to help train future filmmakers. Built in 1937 by Dixon Scott, great uncle of film directors Ridley and Tony Scott, the Tyneside is the finest surviving purpose-built news theater in Britain, and Newcastle's only full-time arts cinema. The 'Coffee Rooms' on the second floor are a local institution which has been in operation since the 1930s and remains a popular place to meet. The award-winning project has attracted a wider audience to the cinema, increasing attendance by 70 percent.

PROJECT FACTS

Address: 10 Pilgrim Street, Newcastle upon Tyne, NE1 6QG, United Kingdom. **Conservation architect:** Cyril Winskell MBE. **Client:** Tyneside Cinema. **Completion:** 2008. **Original building:** 1937 by Dixon Scott. **Number of seats:** 544. **Largest screen diameter:** 4.5 m. **Sound equipment:** Dolby sound system. **Kind of projection:** 35 mm, 2 k digital projectors. **Additional functions:** digital film production, editing suites. **Main materials:** exterior: terracotta, glazed bricks, polycarbonate, zinc; interior: plaster mouldings, glass mosaic floors. **Setting:** urban.

↑ | **New roof extension**
← | **Restored Newreel Theatre** with the original color scheme reinstated

← | **Current building section**

↓ | **Decoration** reflecting Dixon Scott's obsession with eastern ornament

Chapman Taylor
Czech Republic

↑ | **Audience,** red upholstered seats
→ | **Foyer** with small seating area, café/bar

Cinema City

Pilsen

Cinema City is located at the heart of Pilsen, 80 kilometers west of Prague. It is part of the Pilsen Plaza shopping center, and with 2,200 square meters, is the largest multiplex in town. The aim of the project was to create a high quality interior featuring unique, dynamic lighting combined with captivating details. The foyer is dominated by a black ceiling with indirect red lighting and a contrasting yellow tunnel which leads to the cinema entrances. The blue-lit ticket area is clad in Alucobond and has a rounded end wall which supports illuminated film display panels. The foyer has a small seating area with café/bar serving light refreshments.

PROJECT FACTS

Address: Shopping Centre Plzen Plaza, Radcicka 2, 301 00 Pilsen, Czech Republic. **Cinema shell and core architects:** Y. Y. Granot Architects. **Client:** IT International Theathers. **Completion:** 2008. **Number of seats:** 1,720. **Additional functions:** café and light refreshments bar. **Setting:** inner city.

↑ | **A contrasting yellow tunnel** leading from foyer to different cinema entrances

↓ | **Elevation**, foyer

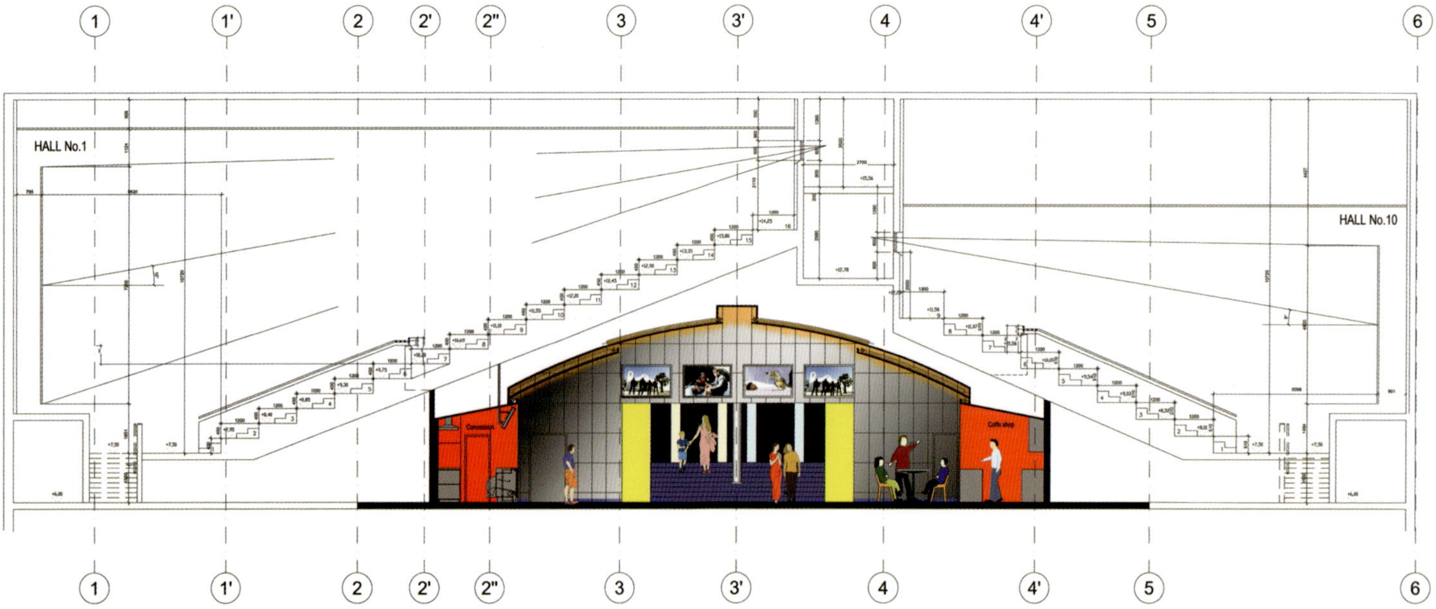

← | **Detail,** foyer dominated by black ceiling with indirect red lighting
↙ | **Corridor**

Robert Majkut Design

↑ | Premiere hall
↗ | The main entrance
→ | The main foyer

Multikino Golden Terraces

Warsaw

The Golden Terraces, Poland's best-known commercial center, is also the most spectacular, stylish, elegant and chic cinema in the heart of Warsaw. A total design has been created, covering the entire complex and all image-related aspects of visual identification like the logo, cinema guides, popcorn boxes and other graphical elements. There are three levels: The main foyer and seven auditoria, the Velvet Bar and the "35mm" music club. Thanks to modern technological solutions such as one of the biggest screen in Europe, "Christie", a world-class digital projector, and the "Martin Audio" sound system, all placed in the center of impressive design arrangements, one can fully experience the magic of the cinema world.

PROJECT FACTS

Address: Ul Złota 59, 00-120 Warsaw, Poland. **Client:** GRUPA ITI. **Completion:** 2007. **Number of seats:** all audiences: 2,551; main audience: 777. **Largest screen diameter:** 28.2 m. **Sound equipment:** Martin Audio. **Kind of projection:** Christie digital projector. **Additional functions:** Velvet bar, "35mm" music club and bar. **Setting:** inner city.

↑ | Box-office

↙ | First floor plan

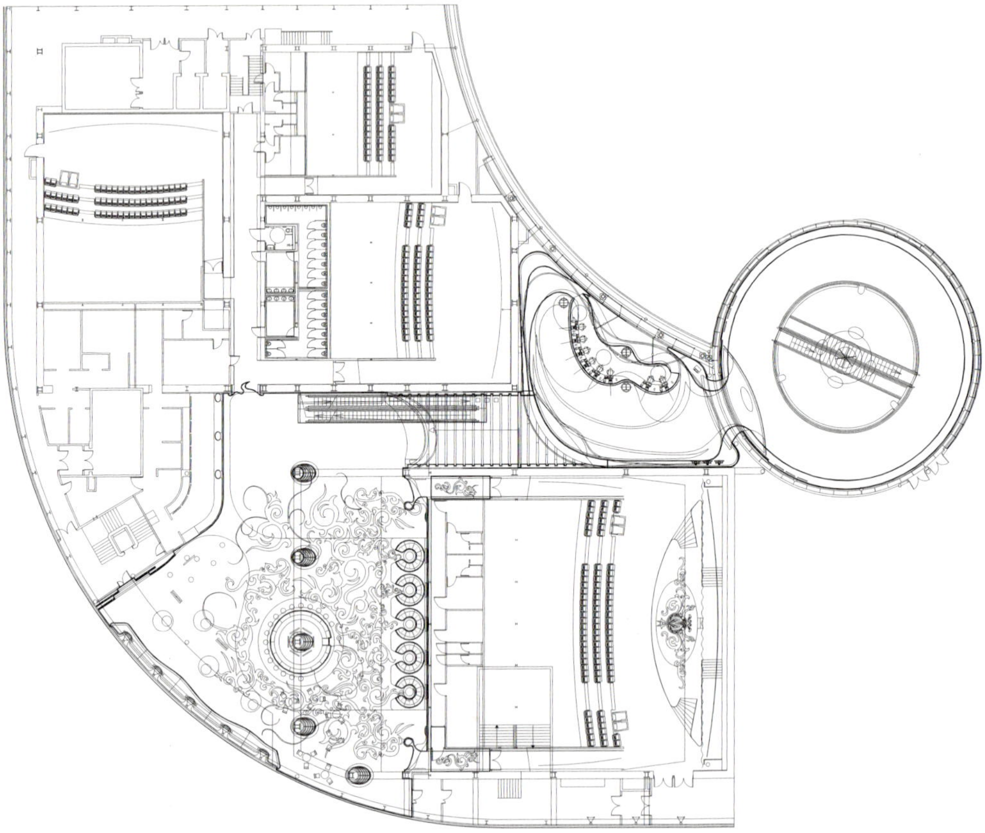

← | **"35mm" music club**, on the third floor
↓ | **Velvet bar**

Soeters Van Eldonk architecten

↑ | **Main entrance cinema**
→ | **Main entrance** at dusk

Pathé Cinema De Kuip

Rotterdam

On the former Piet Smit dockyard between the Maas River and the busy boulevard near the Feyenoord Stadium, large-scale commercial functions are being combined with housing. The master plan, designed in association with Rudy Uytenhaak, is centered around a long strip accommodating commercial functions, turned away from the thoroughfare; behind it is a zone of residential buildings and plazas. In addition to large retail venues, the commercial strip also houses a cinema and a police station, and was designed as a single cohesive architectural and urban design entity, interrupted only by accesses to the residential area. It holds an additional function of a sound buffer for the residential neighborhood.

PROJECT FACTS

Address: Cor Kieboomplein 501, 3077 MK Rotterdam, The Netherlands. **Client:** Pathé Theatres BV. **Completion:** 2002. **Number of seats:** 2,746. **Largest screen diameter:** 20.08 m. **Sound equipment:** Dolby, SRD, DTS. **Kind of projection:** 35 mm and digital. **Main materials:** exterior: corrugated steel; interior: corrugated steel, plasterboard. **Setting:** urban.

↑ | **View into the foyer**

← | **Foyer,** view from first floor

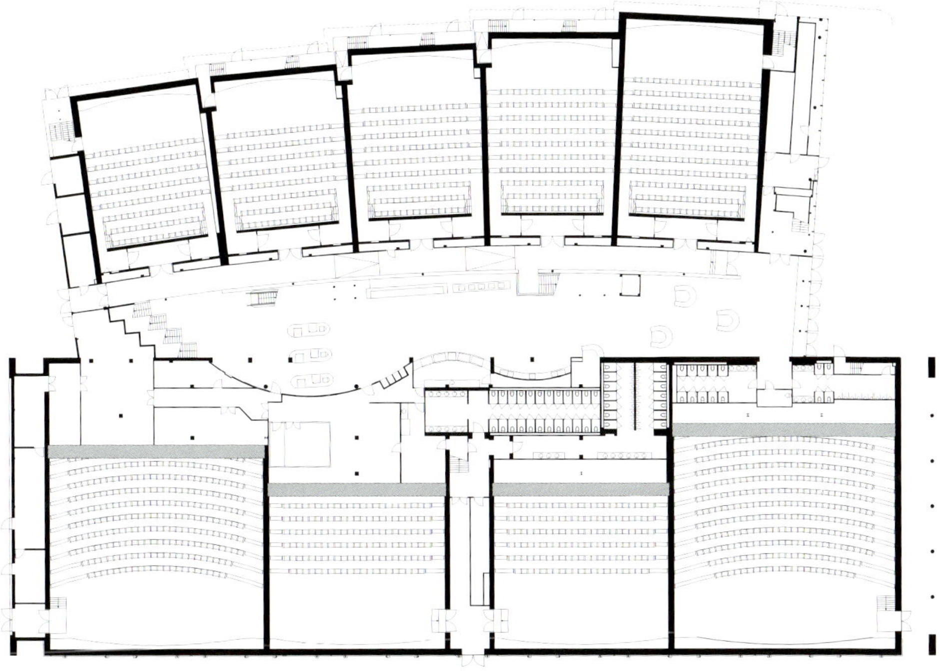

← | **Plan**
↓ | **Foyer**, view from second floor

Maarten Douwe Bredero

↑ | General view
↓ | Different elevations

Cinema Space

Hengelo

As an asymmetrical envelope, the building is carefully positioned on this former downtown parking lot with ample room for firemen and visitors to the adjacent discotheque. In order to minimize its environmental impact, the height of the building is limited. Moreover, the original open square remains 'unimpaired' by visually continuing the outdoor space into the building and vice versa. The floors are coated with black pigmented concrete encasing stainless steel tubes in a 'Mikado' pattern. Above this transparent area, rooms are accessed on two levels by stairs and an elevator. The open stairway is made of steel and pink glass. One flight up, a single flat-floored L-shaped projection room shows movies on five screens. The capacity of the rooms, situated side by side, varies from 300 to 100 viewers.

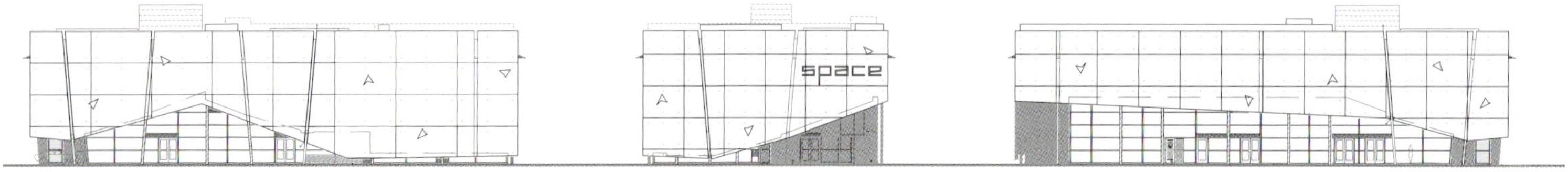

PROJECT FACTS

Address: Beekstraat 41, 7551 DP Hengelo, The Netherlands. **Client:** Bioscooponderneming Bellevue. **Completion:** 2005. **Number of seats:** 850. **Largest screen diameter:** 15 m. **Sound equipment:** analog/ THX (partly). **Kind of projection:** 35 mm/digital (partly). **Additional functions:** café. **Main materials:** exterior: concrete, hardwood, glass; interior: concrete, cloth, spray. **Setting:** inner city.

↑ | **View of café façade,** glazings on ground level melt interior and surroundings

↑ | **Façade detail**

↓ | **Interior view,** foyer and counter

Page + Steele,
IBI Group Architects

↑ | **Entrance**, general view
→ | **Entrance** with sheltered portico

Cineplex Odeon Queensway

Etobicoke

This complex is the largest of a series of stadium-type theaters designed by Page + Steele. The intent of these cinemas was to create a new entertainment experience by combining unobstructed stadium seating and advanced sound systems with a wide range of food services and entertainment options. Essentially a series of large black boxes, the cinemas were carefully massed and designed to lead towards a broad, sheltered main Art Deco-inspired entrance proscenium. On the interior, oversize curvaceous columns lead towards a theatrical space enhanced by a computer controlled sound and light show. The Queensway complex represents complete design, including the landscape theme, the interiors, concessions, graphics, theme tower and the building itself.

PROJECT FACTS

Address: 1025 The Queensway, Etobicoke, Ontario, Canada. **Interior Design:** Design Corp. **Client:** Cineplex Odeon. **Completion:** 2001. **Number of seats:** 4,556. **Largest screen diameter:** 24.07 m. **Sound equipment:** THX standard. **Additional functions:** VIP lounges, party rooms, Cinemascape Arcades. **Main materials:** exterior: steel, wood, cast plaster. **Setting:** urban.

↑ | Colonnade to central dome

← | View towards ticket counter

← | Seating area and concessions
↓ | Site plan

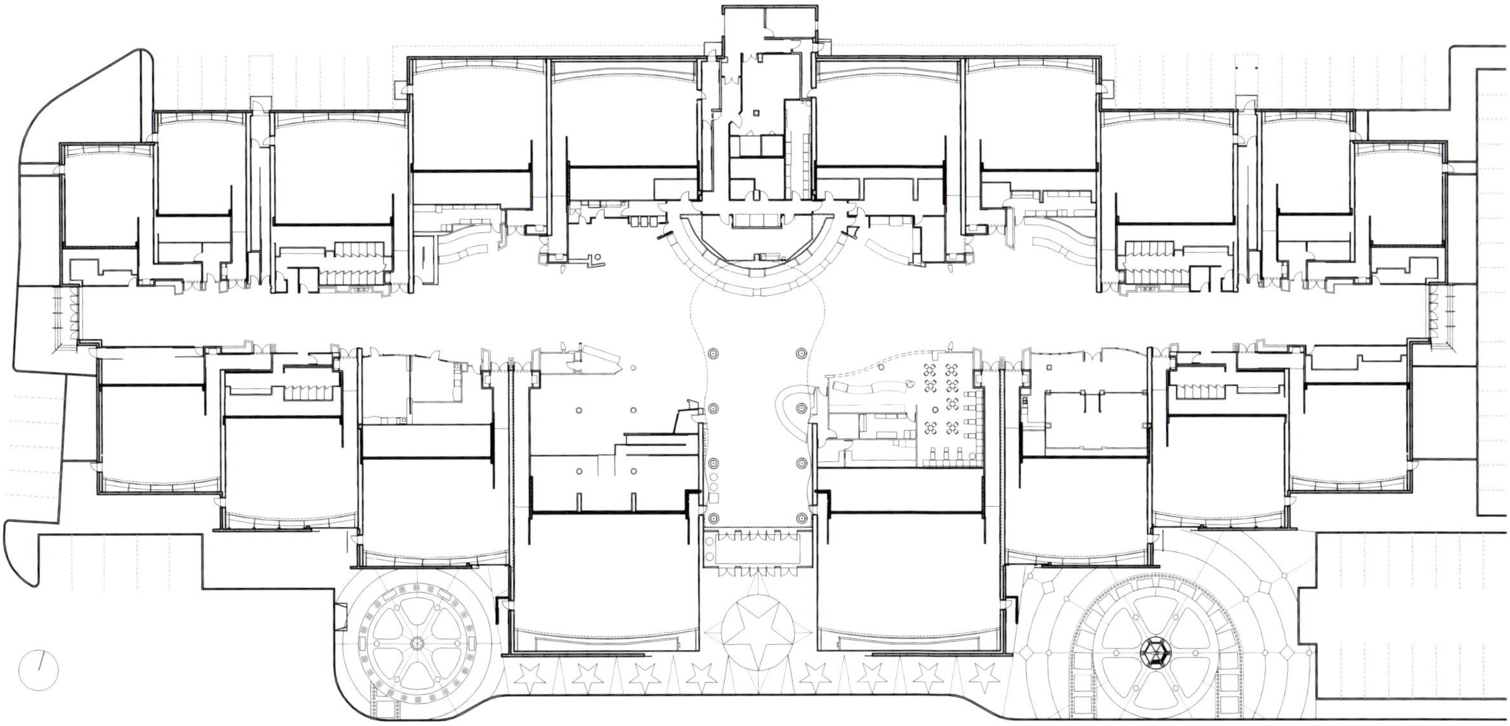

Andrea Viviani Architects

↑ | **Interior view,** foyer

Cinecity Udine

Pradamano

The multiplex is a technological cavern, a new concept of space, both primordial and modern. At night, it projects its glow through the hundred fluorescent bodies positioned inside the metal canopy of the entrance front. Only the restaurant's large high rectangle of glazed panels breaks down the long brick-red ribbon of the building. Inside, everything is warm and shining: from the floor with back-lit cut-outs to the lighting channel on the wall and floor of the access corridor. Daylight filters in four different colors from façade panes. Dark shades dominate the rest of the complex, from shiny black iron elements to the chocolate tones in the corridor walls and flooring.

PROJECT FACTS

Address: Via Nazionale, s.s. 56, 33040 Pradamano, Italy. **Site Engineer:** Marco Roboni. **Engineer:** Gianni Rossato. **Client:** Furlan cinemas & theatres. **Completion:** 2002. **Number of seats:** 2,500. **Largest screen diameter:** 24.6 m. **Sound equipment:** electrovoice. **Kind of projection:** Christie digital projector, analog (barco-cinemeccanica). **Main materials:** exterior: prefabricated concrete panels, coloured scraped rendering; interior: plasterboard, concrete, steel. **Setting:** suburban.

↑ | **Ground floor plan**
↓ | **Entrance corridor** to the theaters

↑ | **Front elevation**
↓ | **Distribution corridor** to the theaters

Andrea Viviani Architects

↑ | **Main foyer** with bar area
→ | **Vertical distribution,** staircase

Cinecity Padova

Limena

The multiplex acts as a catalyst which distills and translates the urban landscape of advertising posters, gray industrial warehouses and kaleidoscopic malls, and becomes the symbol of this landscape. The relationship between the artificial and the natural is put into question. Green stains on gray patches of prefabricated panels creased by a relief of tree trunks are replaced by okume wood on the front side panels, conquering the main front and turning it into a hedge of climbing jasmine. Inside, the artificial prevails, and the nature turns into pure ornament. Colors, mirrors and lights look as if their intention is to ensnare the visitor. The interior aims to trigger reactions, which are usually reserved to ambiguity and contradiction-prone contemporary art.

PROJECT FACTS

Address: Via Breda, 35010 Limena, Italy. **Site Engineer:** Marco Roboni. **Engineer:** Gianni Rossato. **Client:** Furlan cinemas & theatres. **Completion:** 2002. **Number of seats:** 3,178. **Largest screen diameter:** 26.8 m. **Sound equipment:** electrovoice. **Kind of projection:** Christie digital projector, analog (barco-cinemeccanica). **Main materials:** exterior: prefabricated concrete panels, polycarbonate, green façade; interior: plasterboard, concrete, polycarbonate. **Setting:** suburban.

↖ | **Main distribution,** corridor
↑ | **Second level,** upper foyer
← | **Main foyer,** entrance restrooms
↓ | **Longitudinal section**

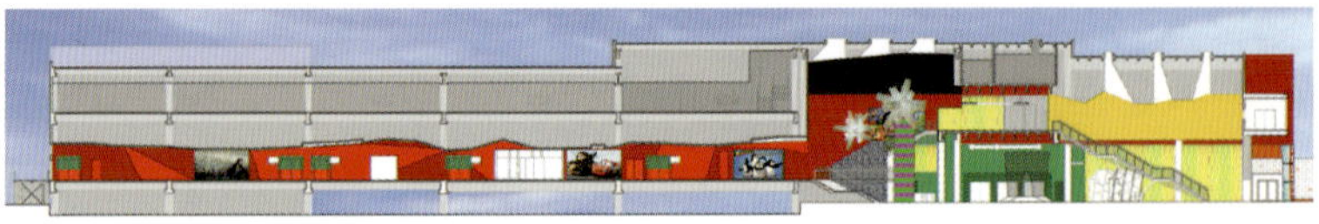

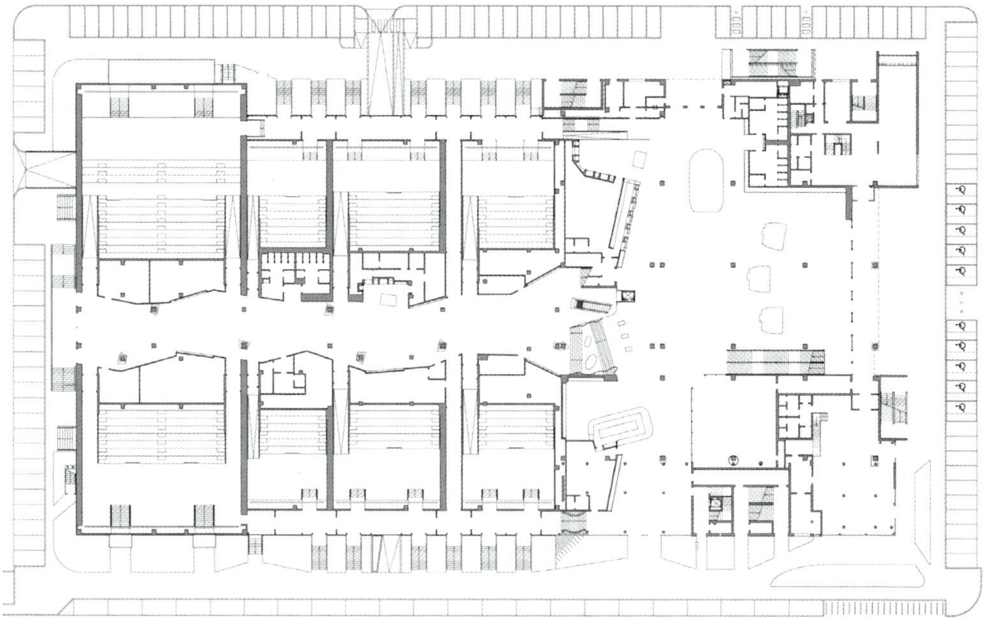

← | **Ground floor plan**
↓ | **Front elevation,** the jasmine façade

Kaup + Wiegand Architekten

↑ | Audience 1
→ | Audience 3

Hackesche Höfe Film Theater

Berlin

Inner courtyards define the urban fabric of Berlin. Within this tradition, Hackesche Höfe – built 1906 in art-nouveau style and at the time europe's largest courtyard-complex – are unique with nine theme-courts of distinct quality, ranging from lively and public to quiet and residential. The secret behind the success of the famous complex lies in recreating the original mix of uses: A modern art-house cinema was installed around the historic theater-court. Foyer, restaurant and bar with view towards court stand right next to contained projection-halls of ‚neutral' appearance. Historical detail and modern technology fully visible, flexible acoustic panels account for perfect THX-standard within former ballrooms and landmark façades.

PROJECT FACTS

Address: Rosenthaler Straße 40/41, 10178 Berlin, Germany. **Original building:** August Endell, 1906/07. **Client:** Timebandits GmbH & Co KG. **Completion:** 2005. **Number of seats:** all audiences: 790; main audience: 325. **Largest screen diameter:** 11 m. **Sound equipment:** THX-standard. **Additional functions:** restaurant, bar. **Setting:** inner city.

↖ | **Projection machine room**
↑ | **Lounge,** stairs
→ | **Foyer**
↙ | **Third floor plan**

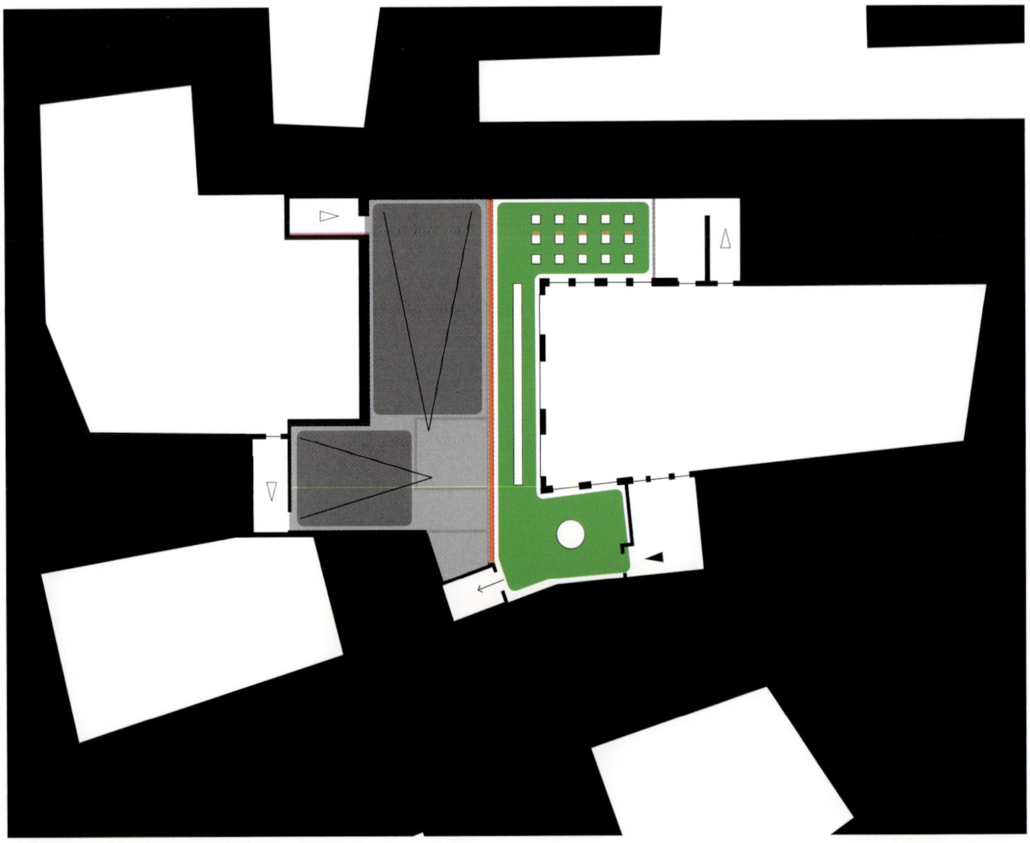

GRÄFIN

Lorenz + Partner

↑ | **Corner,** with staircase and pillars bearing the new structure above the old building

CinemaxX

Hamburg

The cinema completes the development of the Quarree Wandsbek Market shopping center. Due to missing open space, it was erected on a 102-meter spanning bridge structure positioned on the complex's roof, a unique feat for Europe. In order to leave the retail operation undisturbed during the construction period, it was decided against building a central circulation, which would have pierced through all levels of the mall. Even though today, spans of over 100 meters are technically possible, mounting a spatial steel framework with a 102-meter long, 16-meter high main beam, weighing ca. 700 tons, presented a logistical challenge.

PROJECT FACTS

Address: Quarree 8–10, 22041 Hamburg-Wandsbek, Germany. **Client:** B+L Immobilien AG. **Completion:** 2000. **Number of seats:** all audiences: 1,411, main audience: 502. **Largest screen diameter:** 20.30 m. **Sound equipment:** Dolby Digital Sound. **Main materials:** exterior: steel; interior: drywall. **Setting:** urban.

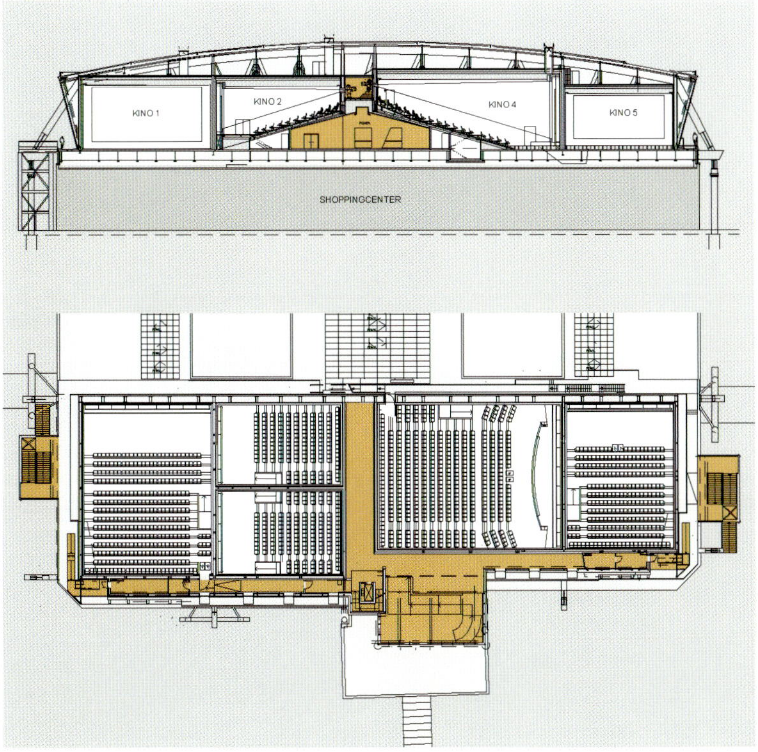

↑ | **Section and floor plan**

↑ | **Detail,** load-bearing system
↓ | **CinemaxX on shopping-mall Quarree**

arb Architekten / Kathrin Eichenberger, Christine Odermatt

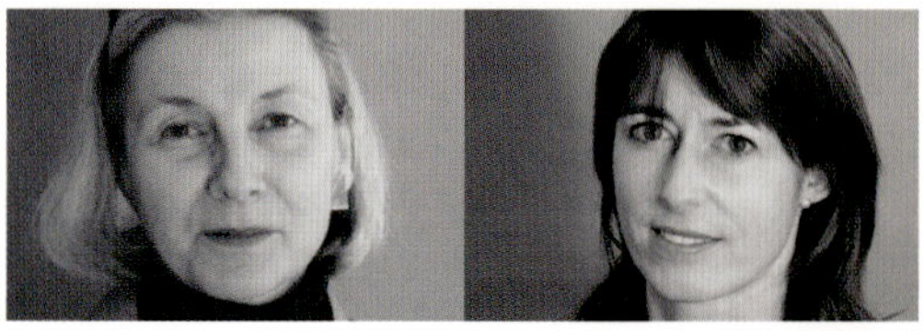

↑ | **Bar** downstairs
↗ | **Main auditorium**
→ | **Ticket counter** and staircase with frosted mirrors

Cinema Bubenberg

Berne

The pre-planned project for the reconstruction of the Bubenberg house predetermined the appearance of the cinema: the narrow foyer area is positioned on the street and the below-ground level behind the street façade, the theater is placed between the fire partition walls below street level. It was attempted to create attractive cinema vestibules in a space built for a different program. Visitors enter through a glazed arch into a light foyer, where a view into the structure's depth opens up to them. This is a staging of a light show, which leads the cinema guests through the various spatial layers from the real world into the theater.

PROJECT FACTS

Address: Laupenstrasse 7, 3011 Berne, Switzerland. **Akustics:** Grolimund + Partner AG. **Client:** Beautiful Films AG. **Completion:** 2000. **Largest screen diameter:** 13.16 m. **Sound equipment:** THX-standard. **Kind of projection:** Cinemeccanica Victoria 8. **Additional functions:** bar. **Main materials:** exterior: sandstone; interior: glass, steel mesh, frosted mirrors. **Setting:** inner city.

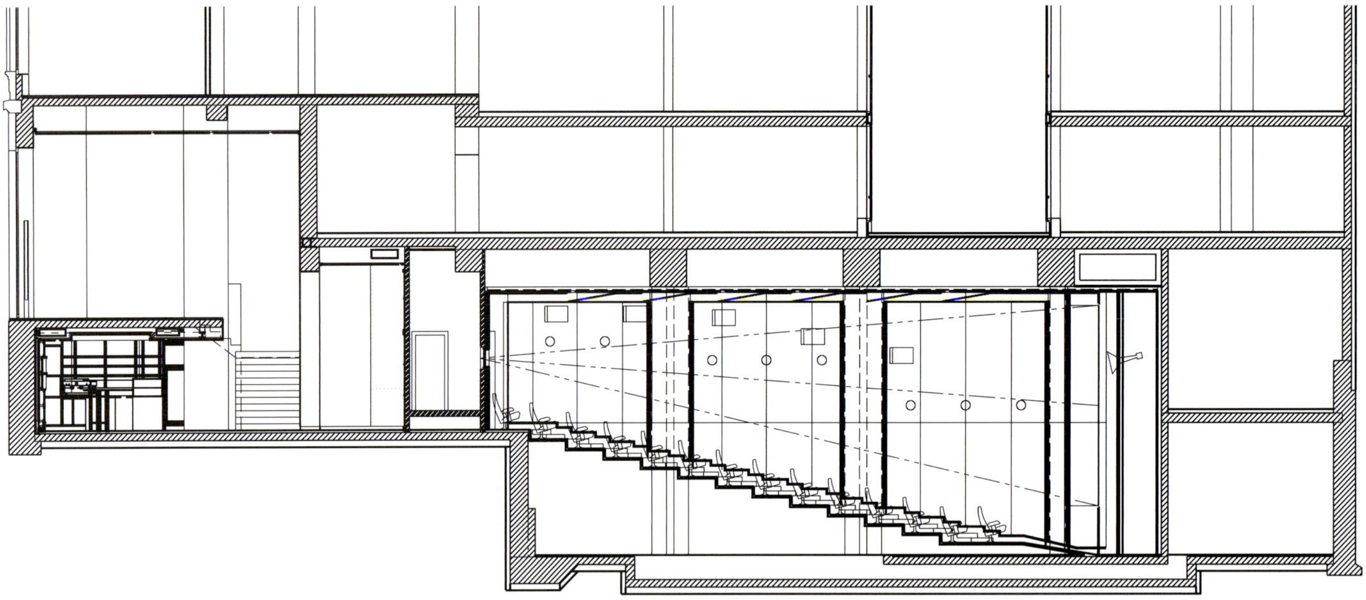

↑ | **Section**
← | **Steel mesh wall**

← | **Stairs** to the audience and bar

↓ | **Basement floor plan**

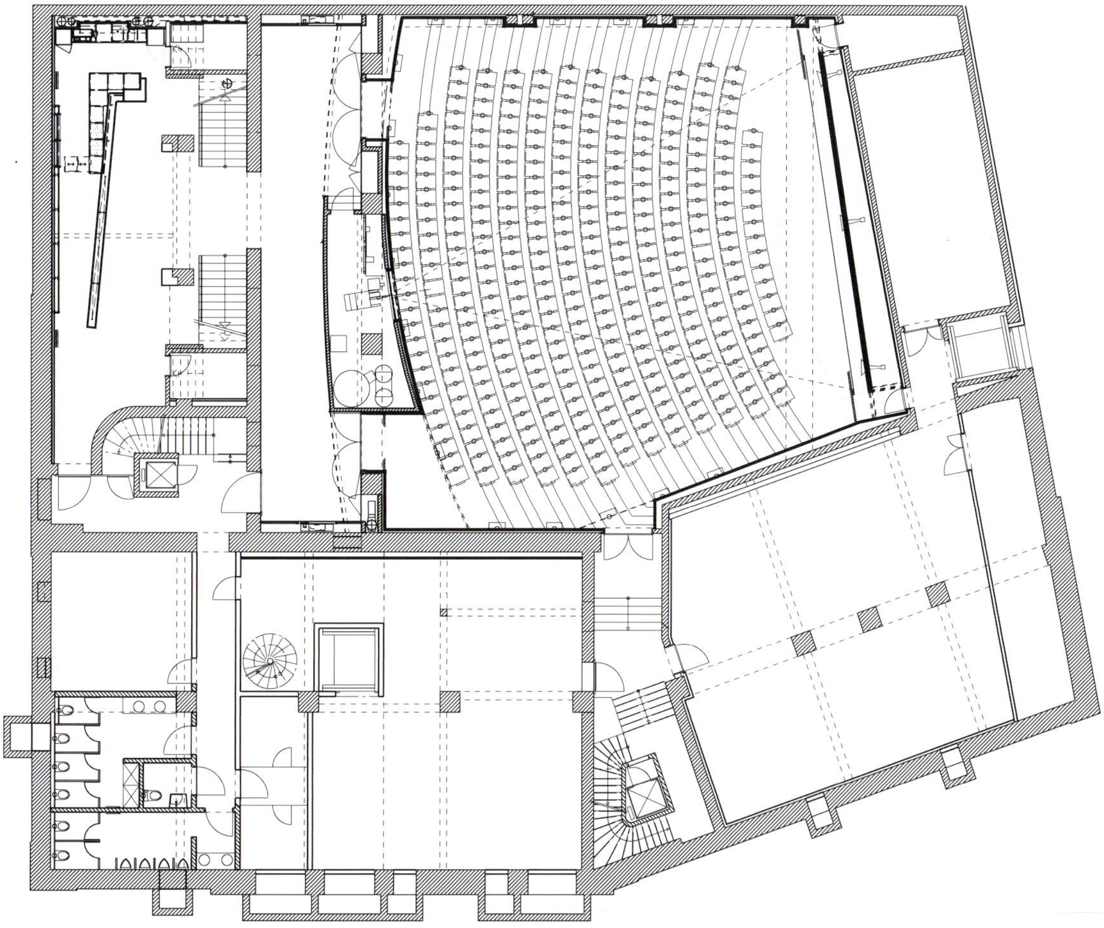

Spot-focus

↑ | Cinema at rooftop

Cinema at Limes Hotel

Fortitude Valley

The design approach focused on the Hotel in its entirety, considering its intended look and feel and paying heavy attention to the interiors, furniture, surfaces and finishes; the design's influence extends even to the Limes' music and drinks list. The façade has been tangibly branded with the Limes logo on a large scale, which is also found on details throughout the hotel lobby, rooms and the rooftop bar and cinema. The rooftop displays a well-balanced design which invites guests to enjoy a drink in the sun at daytime and turns into a movie and entertainment area in the evening hours. With the city lights serving as a background, a very special movie experience is made possible.

PROJECT FACTS

Address: 142 Constance St., Fortitude Valley, QLD 4006, Australia. **Planning Partner:** Kevin Hayes Architects, RW Joiners, IDEA creations. **Client:** Damian Griffiths. **Completion:** 2008. **Number of seats:** 25. **Largest screen diameter:** 3 m. **Additional functions:** rooftop bar. **Setting:** inner city.

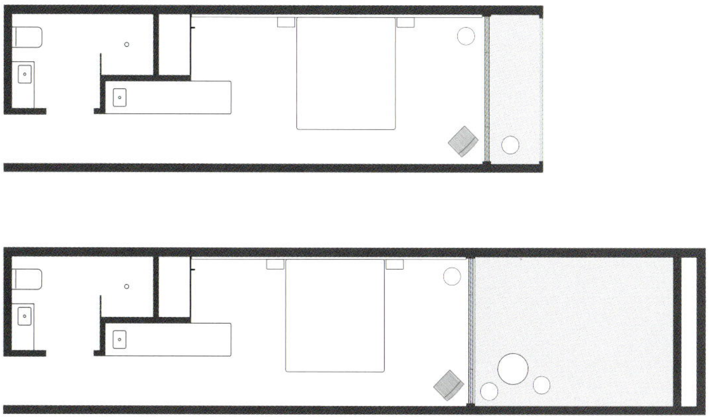

↑ | **Layout plans**

↑ | **Exterior view**

↓ | **Rooftop**, detail view of furnishings

↑ | Interior view

Linked Hybrid

Beijing

The 220,000 square meter complex aims to counter the current urban developments in China by creating a porous space for the 21st century which invites visitors inside and is open to the public from its every facet. It presents a cinematic urban experience of space. The theater's multifaceted spatial layers, as well as its many passages, make the Linked Hybrid an open city within a city. The large urban space in the center is activated by a graywater recycling pond with water lilies and grasses in which the cinematheque and the hotel appear to float. In the winter, the pool freezes over to be transformed into an ice skating rink. The cinematheque's architecture floats in the shallow pond above its own reflection, and projections on its façades reflect the films playing inside.

PROJECT FACTS

Address: 1 Xiangheyuan Road, MOMA Building, Dongcheng District, Beijing 1000028, PR China. **Client:** Modern Green Development Co., Ltd. Beijing. **Completion:** 2009. **Setting:** urban.

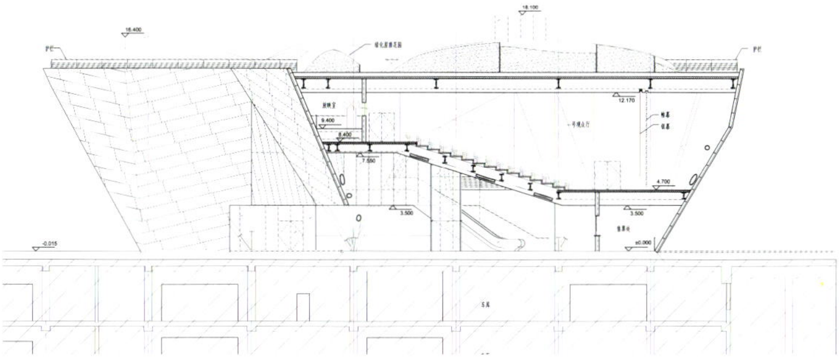

↑ | **Section**
↓ | **Public passages**

↑ | **Façade,** multifaceted spatial layers
↓ | **Public functions** connected to green spaces

↑ | **Skyline Residence at dusk,** view from below
→ | **View from rear yard**

Skyline Residence
Los Angeles

A unique private outdoor cinema is the result of a spatial separation of the main building and the guest house of the Skyline Residence. The space between the two buildings is used both as an auto court and as an open air cinema. This decision was guided by the idea that complimenting forms, which are spatially perceived as belonging to each other, give an interstitial space between them a sense of connection, even if only visually. In this design, the faces resulting from the separation of the forms has created viewing areas for videos and film. The deck above the garage has been designed as a gathering space for social events and a viewing platform for projections onto the southern face of the guest house. All this creates a setting hardly matched by any other cinema in the world.

PROJECT FACTS

Address: Los Angeles, CA, USA. **Interior Design:** Elizabeth Paige Smith. **Client:** Belzberg Architects. **Completion:** 2007. **Largest screen diameter:** 6.71 m. **Sound equipment:** standard exterior grade speakers. **Kind of projection:** front projection. **Additional functions:** private residence, roof deck. **Main materials:** stucco. **Setting:** urban.

↑ | **Viewing platform** and social gathering space above the park deck
← | **Interstitial space** as parquet

← | **Guest house wall** as screen
↓ | **Site plan**

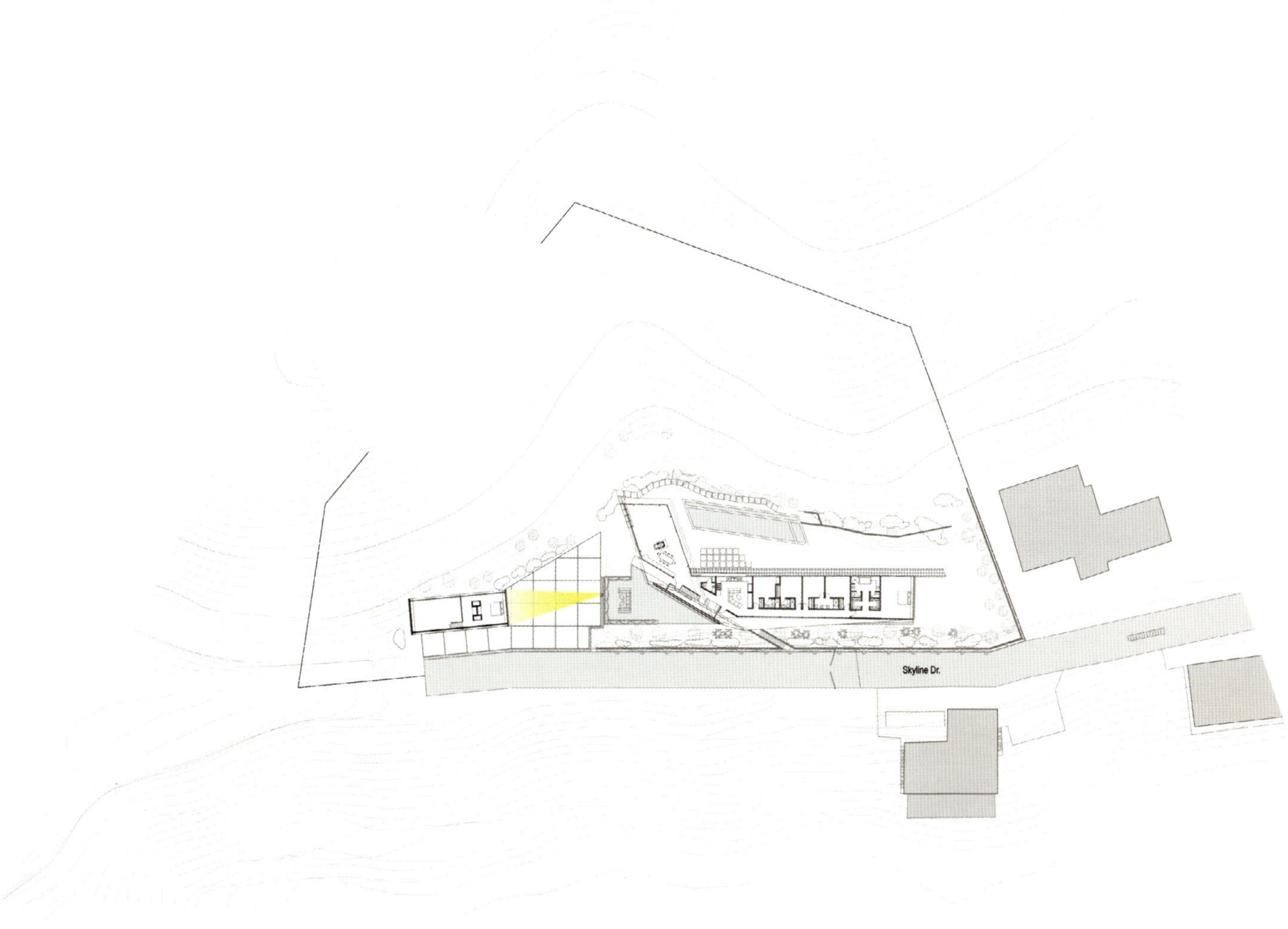

Bureau des Mésarchitectures / Didier Fiuza Faustino

↑ | **Interior,** screen and leather cushions for ten spectators
↗↗ | **Drawings,** constructive system
→ | **Exterior view,** H-Box located in MUDAM Luxembourg

H-Box

anywhere

H-Box is a mobile movie theater, a minimalist architecture composed of modules made of high-resistance lightweight materials allowing it to be easily assembled, disassembled and transported to travel around the world. The 6.5-meter unit designed to accommodate up to ten viewers at a time may be assembled in fewer than twelve hours. By placing the body at the center of the space, where its audible and visible influxes converge, H-Box explores the possibilities of experience-based architecture. This hybrid object is a type of camera obscura – both a shelter hidden from view and a place of heightened awareness, in which the body becomes a sensitive film and a hyper-sensory receptor in one.

PROJECT FACTS

Address: anywhere. **Planning partner:** Philippe Smith (engineering), EURO-SHELTER (construction company). **Client:** Hermès International. **Completion:** 2007. **Number of seats:** 10. **Largest screen diameter:** 3.2 m. **Sound equipment:** Dolby Digital 5.1. **Main materials:** exterior: honeycomb aluminum; interior: acoustic panels.

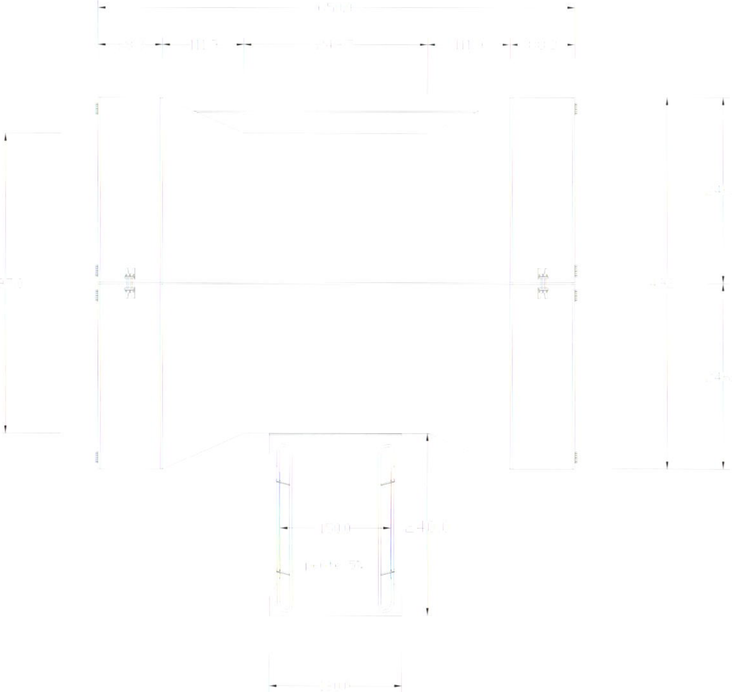

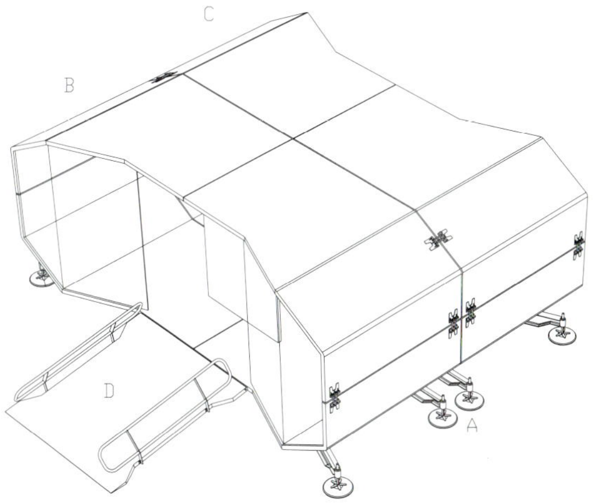

bad architects group with
Sabine Gubi, Julia Kick,
Manuela Kneringer

↑ | **Seating elements** made of fiber-glass reinforced synthetic material, located outdoor throughout the year

Mooskino

Salzburg

In order to transform the Maria-Hilf-Platz in Leopoldskron-Moos on into "Mooskino," an open air cinema for summer evenings, three different seating elements, a partition screen and capes were designed and installed here. The sail-like partition screen protects the cinema atmosphere from the busy street nearby. As an added bonus, its form creates an attractive entrance situation. The specially-developed fleece capes warm movie audiences on cool summer evenings. The seating elements may not only be used during the cinema season, but are present throughout the year as loud, orange eye-catchers in Leopoldskron-Moos. According to the wishes of the district developing association, this project is more than just a cinema, but an enrichment of Salzburg's public space.

PROJECT FACTS

Address: Moosstraße 73, 5020 Salzburg, Austria. **Client:** Association City development Leopoldskron-Moos, Community development Salzburg. **Completion:** 2007. **Number of seats:** 106. **Largest screen diameter:** 8,6 m. **Additional functions:** cityscape intervention. **Main materials:** fiber-glass reinforced synthetic material, PVC Gittermesh, aluminum. **Setting:** suburban.

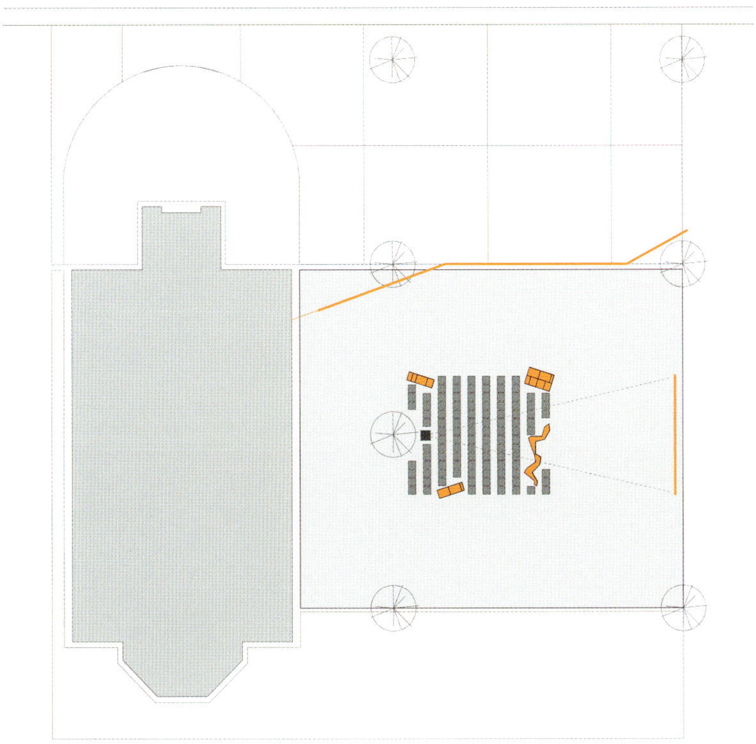

↑ | **Ground floor plan**

↓ | **Night view,** premiere of a movie during a summer evening

↑ | **Seating elements**

BWM Architekten und Partner / Erich Bernard, Daniela Walten, Johann Moser

↑ | **Entrance and café**

Cinema Paradiso

St. Pölten

The cinema offers an entry to the world of films, dreams, adventures, and memories. Unlike television, cinema is a place of common adventure. Cinema Paradiso is a place with a unique identity and atmosphere that plays a vital role in the city center with functions that go far beyond merely showing films as an alternative to television. It is a new kind of cinema offering a mixture of catering, film show, repertory cinema and an open center for arts and culture. The versatile division of spaces creates meeting points for communication and entertainment. The transitions between rooms are seamless and open, supported by color and light.

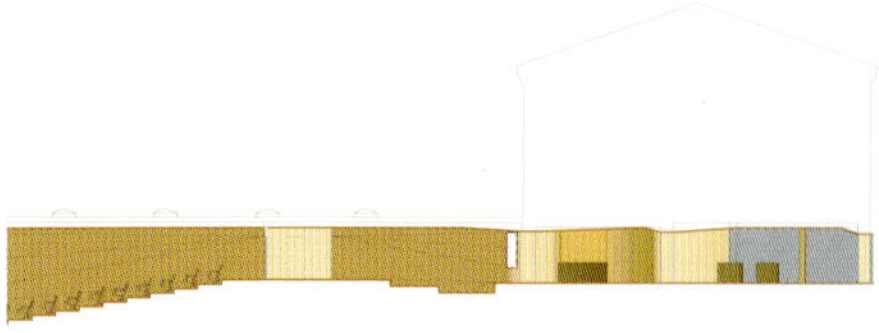

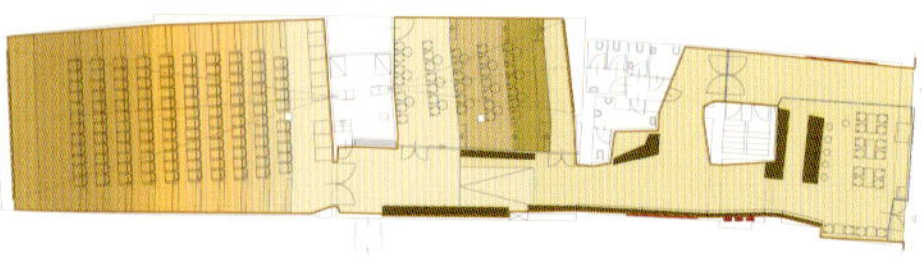

PROJECT FACTS

Address: Rathausplatz 15–S7, 3100 St. Pölten, Austria. **Planning partners:** Erich Bernard, Johann Moser, Erich Klinger, Dolores Kainz, Andreas Tsukalas. **Client:** Verein Cinema Paradiso. **Completion:** 2002. **Number of seats:** 180. **Largest screen diameter:** 8,7 m. **Sound equipment:** Dolby Digital SR. **Kind of projection:** 35 mm, digital. **Additional functions:** open cultural center, bar. **Main materials:** glass. **Setting:** inner city.

↑ | Beislkino
↙ | Section and floor plan

↓ | Foyer

↑ | **Panorama**
↗ | **Family flat roof** on the second floor
→ | **Eastern part** of the north side

Villa Shizilin

Beijing

The client had acquired a piece of land adjacent to the Ming Tombs outside Beijing to build a house with an extensive program extending from a cinema to an indoor swimming pool, with the intention to use the facilities as a club, among others. The building site used to be an orchard for persimmon trees, and is surrounded by mountains. To fully engage the area's scenery, nine tapered spaces are oriented towards nine different views. The slope of the roof is designed to complete these perspective rooms while interpreting traditional Chinese architectural forms in a topological way. The building is constructed using a concrete sheer wall-and-beam system clad with local granite, and dark cement tiles lining the roof.

PROJECT FACTS

Address: Wan Niang Fen, Changping, Beijing, China. **Project Design:** Yung Ho Chang / Wang Hui. **Client:** Antaeus Group. **Completion:** 2003. **Additional functions:** private residence with extensive programs. **Main materials:** concrete and stone load (bearing wall), exposed concrete (ceiling), concrete (tile roof), terrazzo (floor), Corten-steel (veneer). **Setting:** suburban.

↑ | **Main entrance**

← | **Sections**

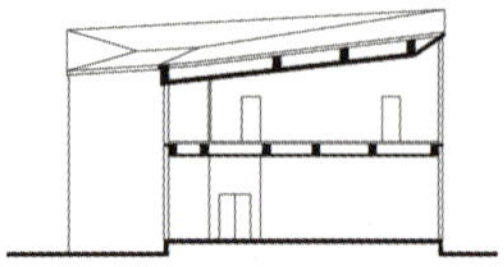

C-C剖面图 1:100
Section C-C

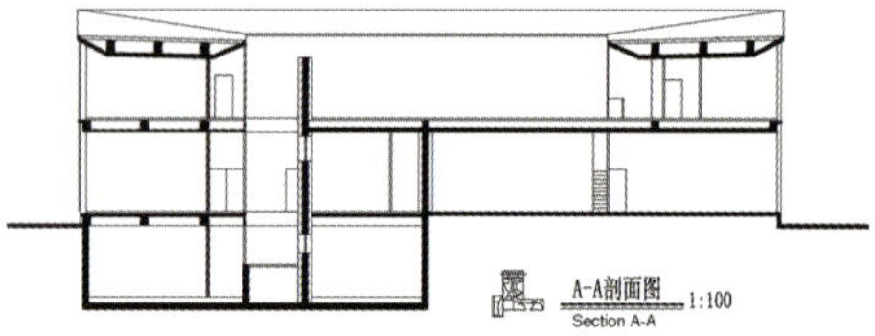

A-A剖面图 1:100
Section A-A

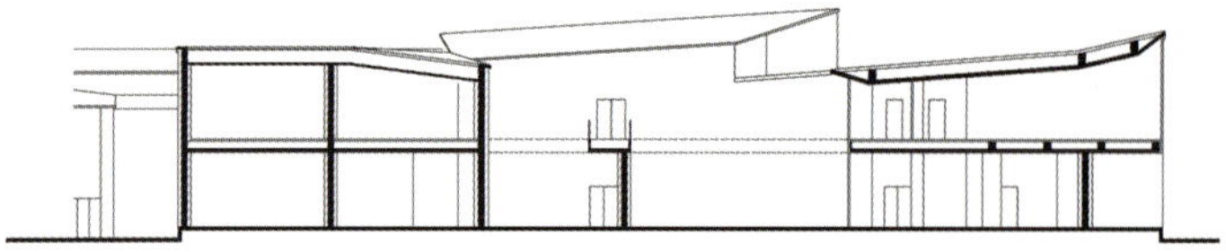

D-D剖面图 1:100
Section D-D

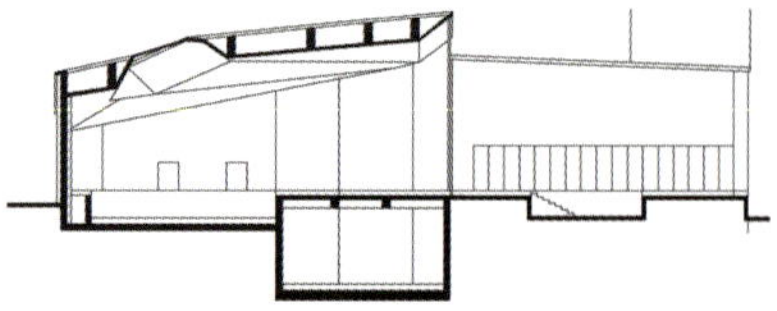

E-E剖面图 1:100
Section E-E

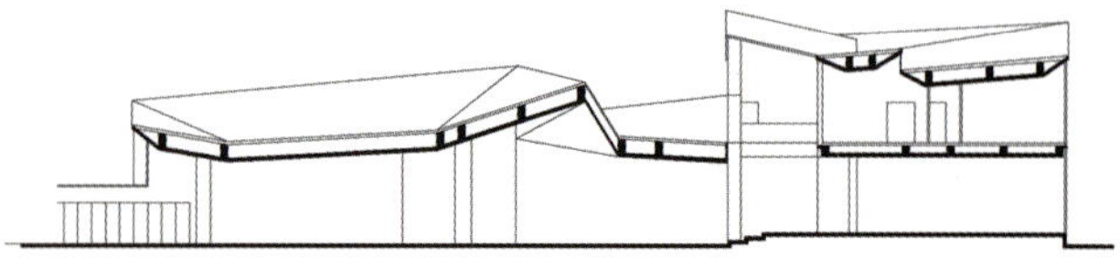

F-F剖面图 1:100
Section F-F

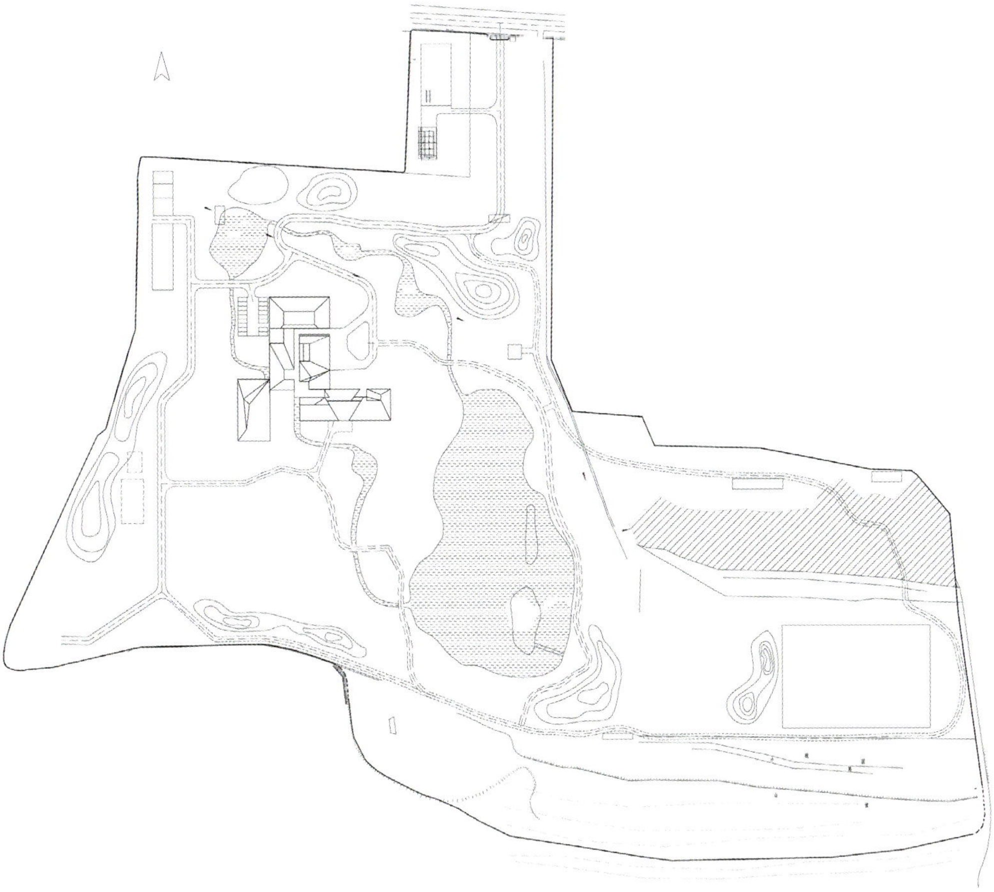

← | **Site plan**
↓ | **Corridor** at ground floor

Hopkins Architects and Expedition Engineers

↑ | **The smallest cinema in the world** on tour in Regent Park

→ | **View through the opened doors** during a screening

Portavilion

London

Portavilion is a portable public art project made of curved plywood, which proves to be a real eye-catcher. Created as part of the London Festival of Architecture 2008, it was utilized in Regents Park and will subsequently be used for further exhibitions around Europe. It is a mobile six-seater cinema which screened a series of films made by the client in the park during the course of a summer. The architects examined historic mobile cinema concepts ranging from caravans with interior seating to vans whose rear doors open to reveal a screen for an exterior 'auditorium'. Made out of wood, the world's smallest cinema has a tiny carbon footprint and is mounted on a steel flatbed trailer.

PROJECT FACTS

Address: Regents Park, London, United Kingdom. **Artist:** Annika Eriksson. **Structural engineer:** ISG InteriorExterior, Wood Newton. **Completion:** 2008. **Number of seats:** 6. **Main materials:** colored curved plywood, steel, carbon. **Setting:** urban.

↖ | **Interior view** during a screening
← | **Four of six seats** and the projector

← | Exterior view
↓ | Sections

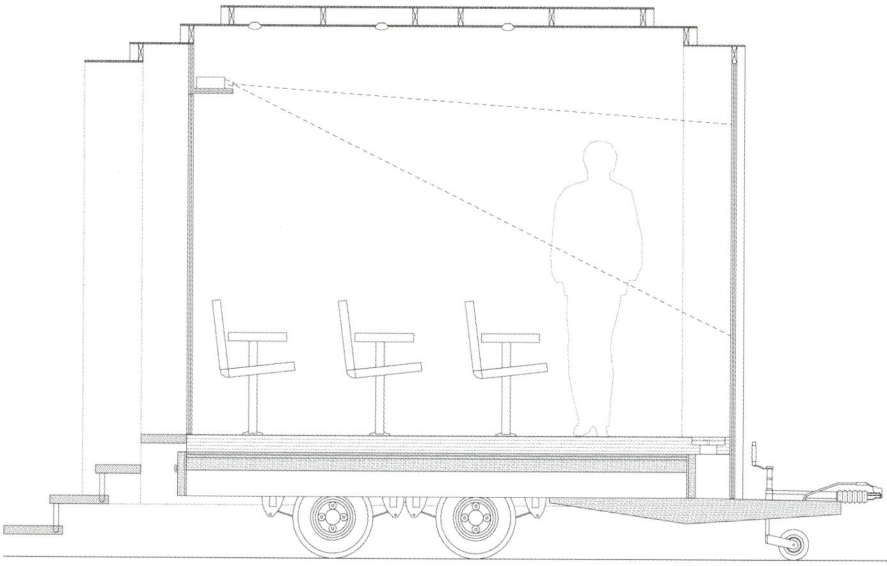

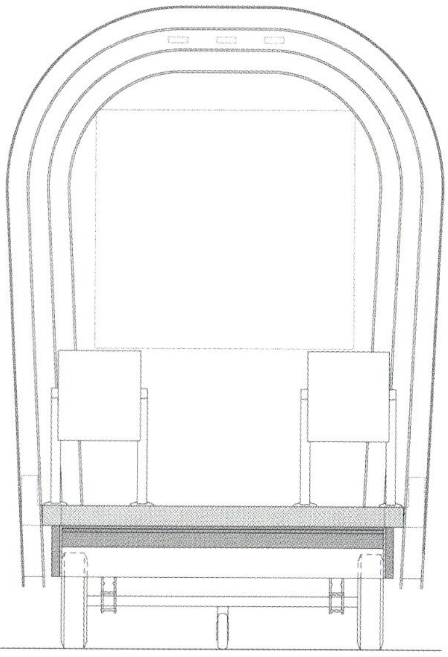

TICK

Multi-focus

Steinmayr & Mascher / Erich G. Steinmayr, Friedrich H. Mascher

↑ | Invisible cinema 3
→ | "Unsicht-Bar"

Austrian Museum of Film

Vienna

The renovation of the cinema with highest esthetic and cinematographic standards created a modern „invisible cinema" as described in theory by Peter Kubelka, co-founder of the museum. A black box without theater illumination is a metaphor for the „head of the movie maker," with the image/box as the eyes, and the sound/speakers as the ears. Neither stage curtains nor opulent decorations distract from this effect. Similar to the bellows of a Lumière camera, the use of black prevents faulty color perception. The architects gradually made the room disappear with highly intelligent planning, while adjusting it to contemporary requirements (seating, escape routes, room and projection technology).

PROJECT FACTS

Address: Augustinerstraße 1, 1010 Vienna, Austria. **Planning partner:** Bernd Heger. **Client:** Österreichisches Filmmuseum. **Completion:** 2005. **Number of seats:** 165. **Largest screen diameter:** 9.5 m. **Sound equipment and kind of projection:** various sound systems and projectors for showing movies from the last century in faithfully original quality. **Additional functions:** museum. **Main materials:** black linoleum floor, black waved stucco walls, black leather, black microfiber. **Setting:** inner city.

↖ | "Unsicht-Bar"
↑ | Foyer
↙ | Bar and ticket counter

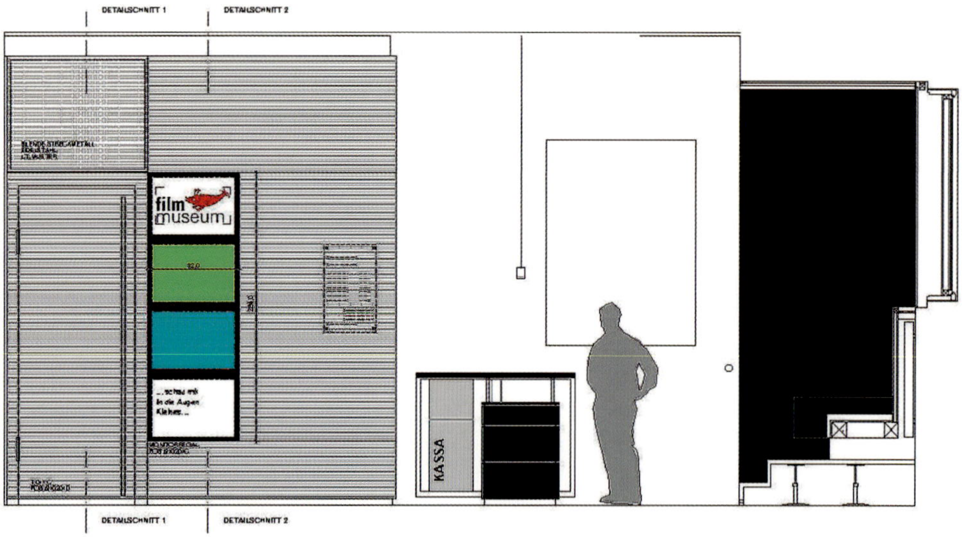

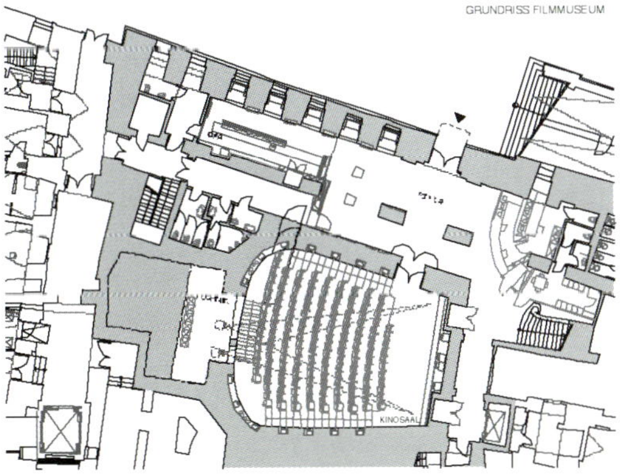

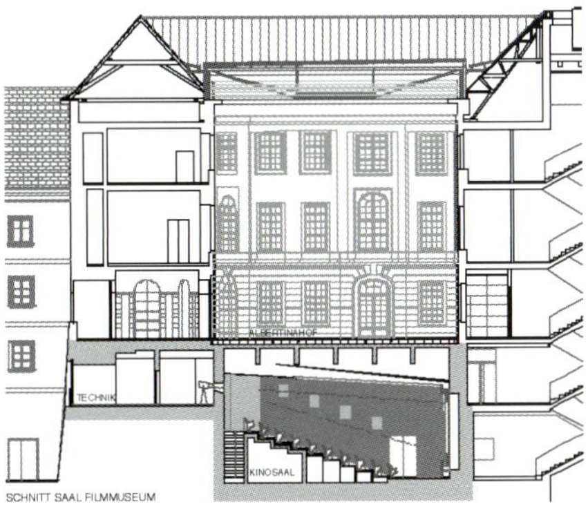

← | Floor plan and section
↓ | Invisible cinema 3

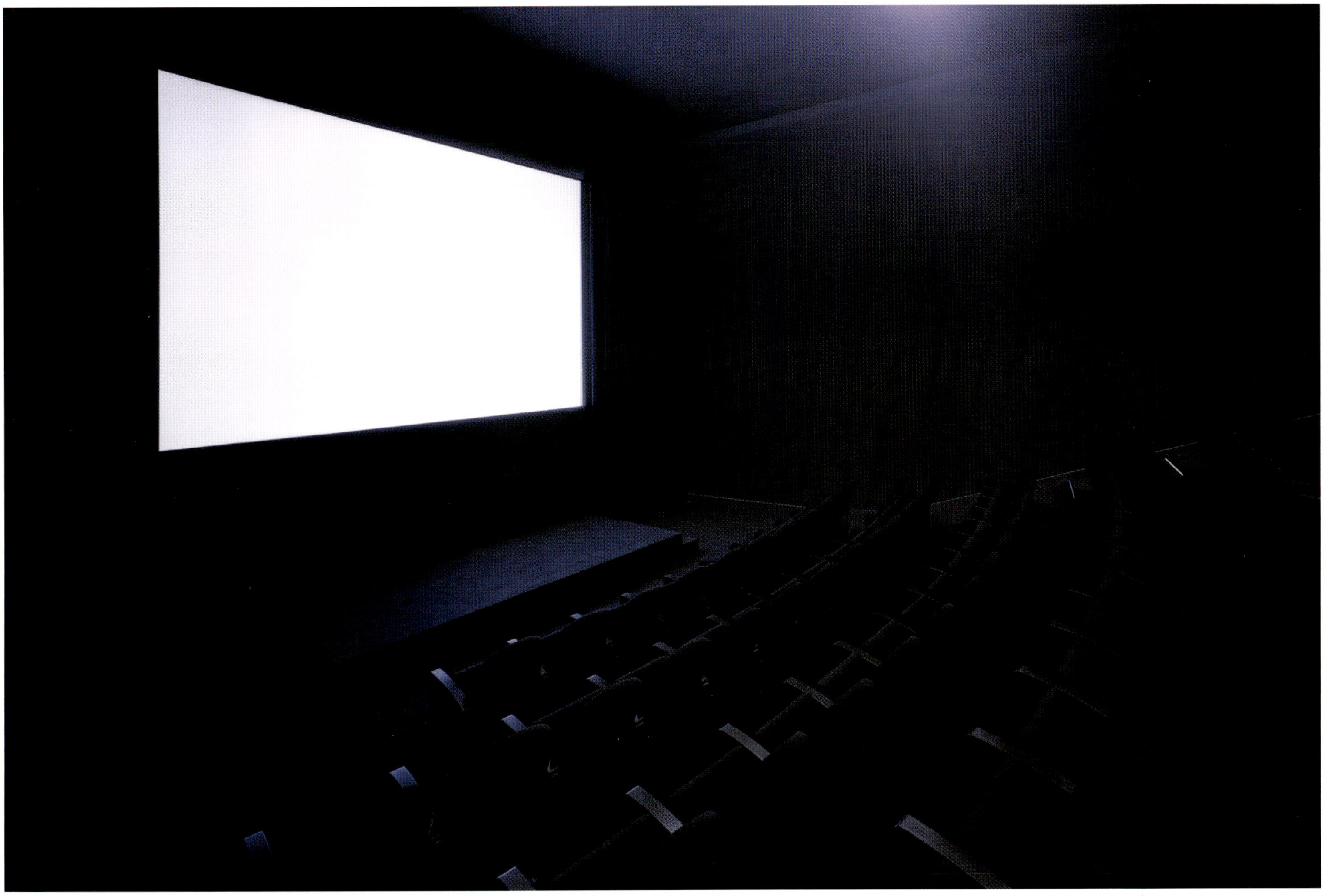

RTKL with Beijing Institute of Architture Design and Rsearch / Xiaoguang Liu

↑ | **Exterior view,** main entrance

↓ | **Section**
↗ | **Front elevation** at dusk
→ | **Interior view,** stairs and IMAX theater

China National Film Museum

Beijing

The China National Film Museum in Beijing came into being as a joint venture of RTKL and the Beijing Institute of Architecture Design and Research, and stands as a tribute to the history and accomplishments of the Chinese film industry. It was part of a ten-monument cultural improvement program initiated by the city for the 2008 Summer Olympics. The design applies a synthetic approach, offering a design language which expresses local experience and maximizes self-sustained integrity, flexibility and environmental friendliness. The museum totals 30,000 square meters and includes exhibition halls, film technology and temporary exhibits, administrative facilities, an IMAX, a 4-D theater and a multi-function hall.

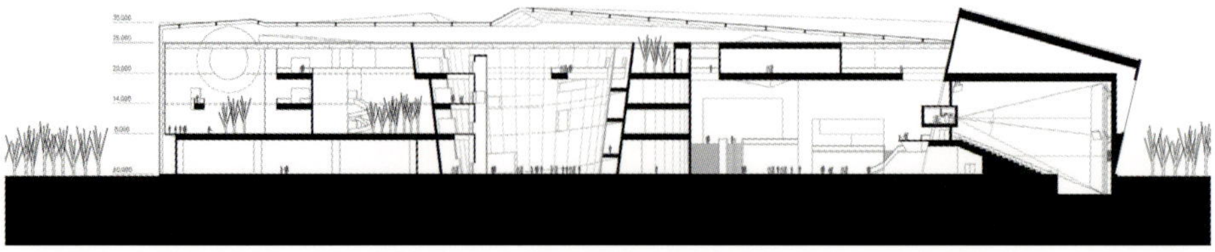

PROJECT FACTS

Address: No. 9, Nan Ying Road, Chaoyang District, 100015 Beijing, China. **Client:** China National Film Museum Project Committee. **Completion:** 2005. **Number of seats:** main audience: 400. **Additional functions:** exhibition space. **Main materials:** exterior: perforated metal panel, metal panel, laminated colored glass; interior: metal panel, tensile fabric, painted drywall, stone and rubber flooring. **Setting:** urban.

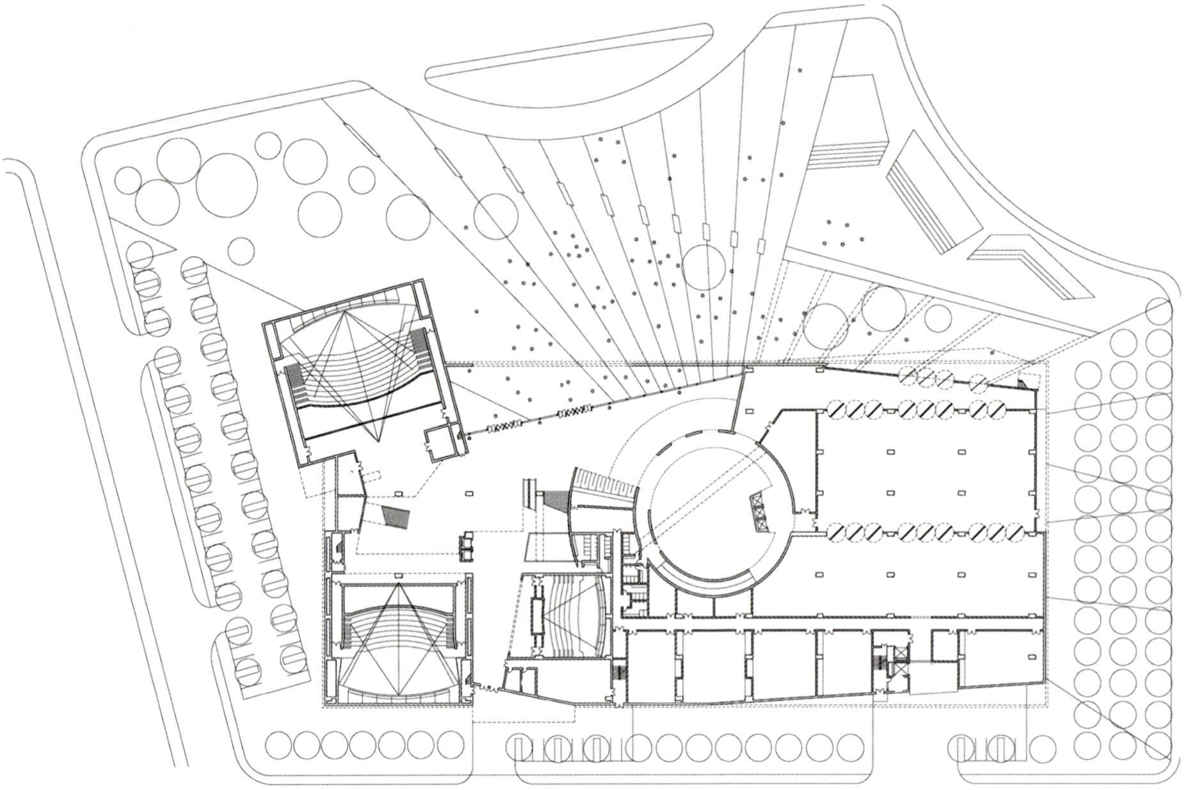

↑ | Ground floor plan
← | Multi-function hall

← | **Lobby at the main entrance**
↓ | **Central hall,** view from ground floor

schmidt hammer lassen architects / John Lassen

↑ | **Total view**
→ | **Exterior view,** showing main entrance and side façade

Culture Island

Middelfart

The sculptural quality of the new Culture Island energizes the newly created peninsula extending from Middelfart's waterfront and is facing the belt where the Lillebælt Bridge connects the island Funen with the mainland of Jutland. For many years, this Danish port city turned its back to the sea, but now the town offers a striking mix of contemporary architecture, culture and the marina beyond. Culture Island is a multi-purpose building which houses several cultural facilities under one roof: a large new library, a cinema, a panoramic restaurant, a café, the tourist information office and a municipal assembly hall. Four large glass panels afford views from the culture center over the water, and also admit generous levels of daylight into the interior. The rest of the façade consists of large surfaces covered with zinc, interrupted by small vertical slits.

PROJECT FACTS

Address: Havnegade 6, 5500 Middelfart, Denmark. **Interior Design:** SHL Architects / Lars Vejen. **Client:** Middelfart Municipality. **Completion:** 2000. **Number of seats:** 350. **Largest screen diameter:** 16 m. **Sound equipment:** Dolby Digital Surround. **Additional functions:** library, café, town hall. **Main materials:** exterior: zinc, glass; interior: plaster, concrete. **Setting:** urban.

← | **Interior view,** restaurant with gallery

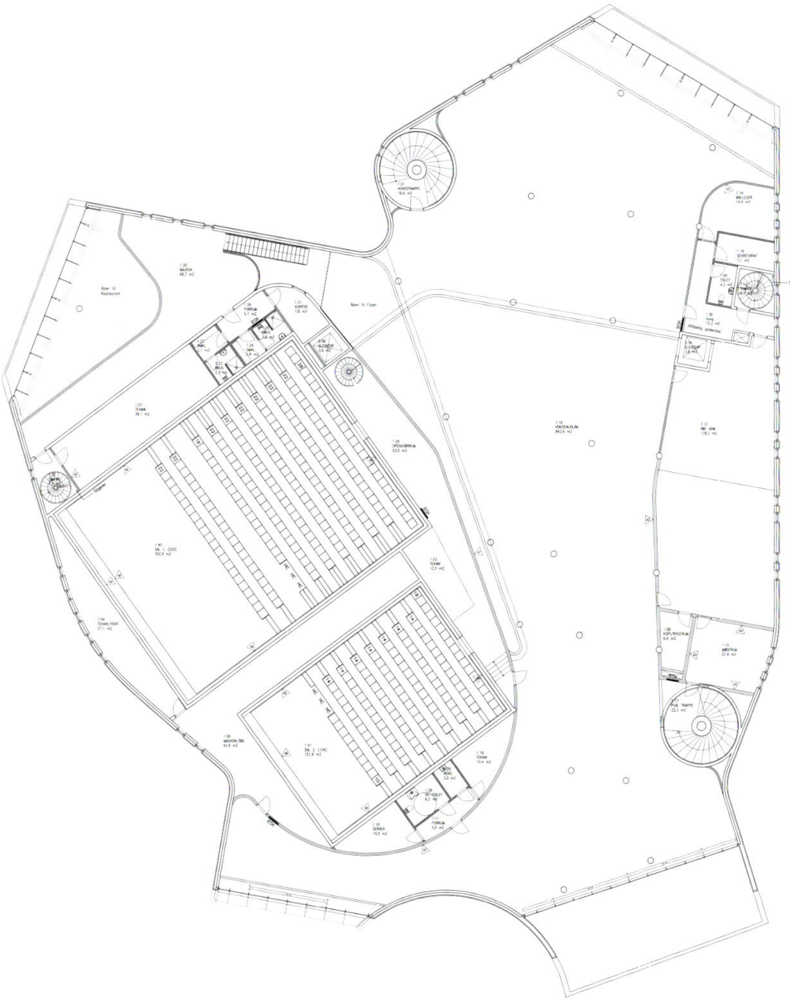

← | **Ground plan**

↓ | **Façade** of glass and zinc at dusk

Franklin Azzi Architecture

↑ | Interior view

Lille 3000

Lille

Lille 3000 is a reconstruction project which turns wasteland around the former Saint Sauveur railway station into a cultural center where screenings, concerts, flea markets and exhibitions can take place. The old station building now shelters a cinema, a bar as well as exhibition spaces. The elegant structures of ashlar brick and iron were restored with respect to the aesthetics of the place while reorganizing spaces and assigning them new functions. The overall design concept combines colorful elements with the gray brickwork of the industrial complex. Inviting spaces inside the building and in the yard create an atmosphere ideal for melting the history of the space with modern culture.

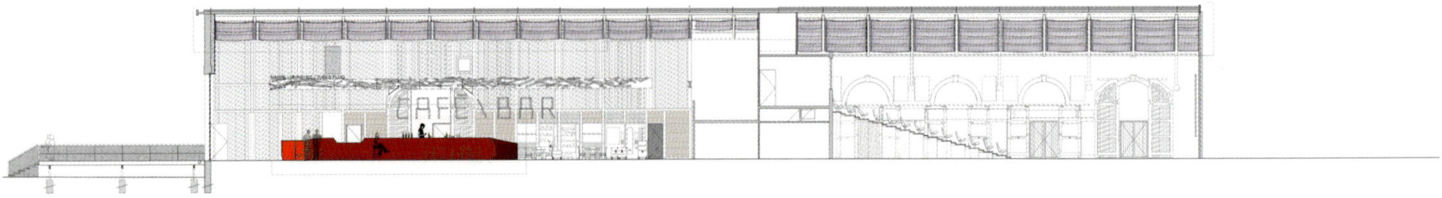

PROJECT FACTS

Address: Gare Saint Sauveur, boulevard Jean Baptiste Lebas, Lille, France. **Interior Design:** Robert Carr. **Client:** Lille 3000. **Completion:** 2009. **Additional functions:** concert location, bar, exhibition space, cinema café, bar. **Main materials:** wood metal, fabric. **Setting:** urban.

↑ | **Exterior view** by night
↙ | **Elevations**

↓ | **Courtyard**

Serero Architects

↑ | **Main entrance**
↗ | **Roof structure** rearticulating the natural surroundings
→ | **Exterior view**

Saint Cyprien Auditorium

Saint Cyprien

The design for the new auditorium and movie theater of Saint Cyprien is inspired by its surroundings. Not only does the body seemingly nestle against the existing buildings, but its façade rearticulates the treetop patterns from the neighboring park. To achieve this natural effect, great care was taken in the auditorium design to reach optimum acoustic quality. The walls are clad with wood slats and the ceiling's complex geometry is able to diffuse sound. In order to allow adaptation of space requirements to different events, the auditorium was divided into seven seating zones of different size. These may be reorganized to achieve the best possible configuration for different uses like movie screenings, concerts, dance events or lectures.

PROJECT FACTS

Address: Les Capellans, 46800 Saint Cyprien, France. **Planning partner:** Beterem Ingénierie, Pasquini acoustics. **Client:** Sud Roussillon municipality. **Completion:** 2011. **Number of seats:** 400. **Largest screen diameter:** 11 m. **Kind of projection:** front projection. **Additional functions:** auditorium, dance theater. **Main materials:** exterior: concrete; interior: wood slats. **Setting:** suburban.

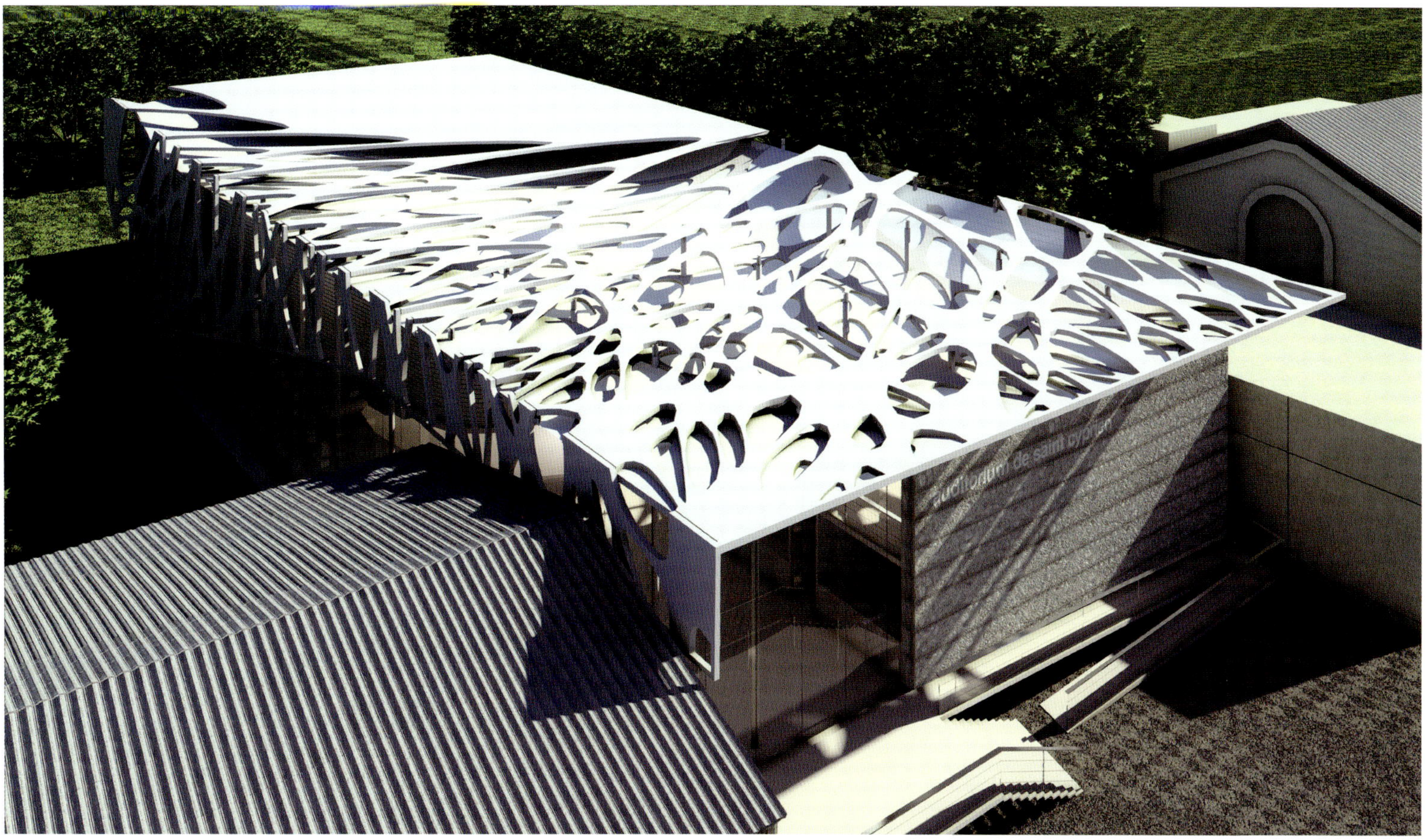

↑ | **Interior view,** foyer
↙ | **Elevations**

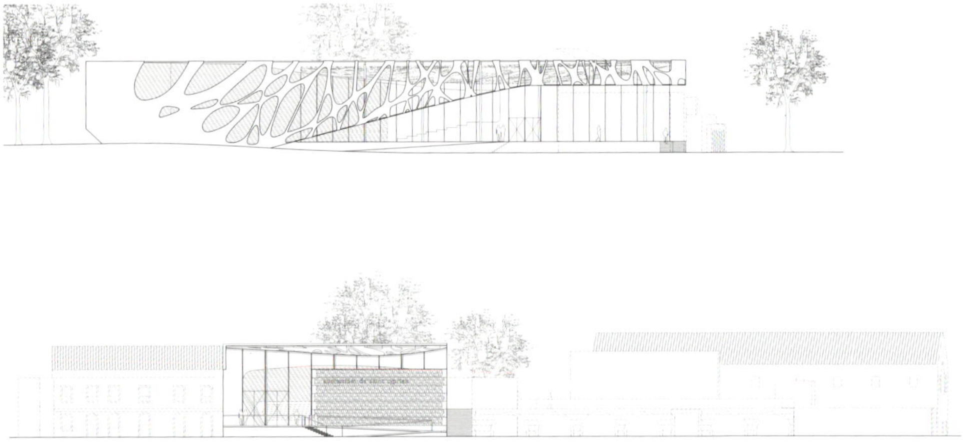

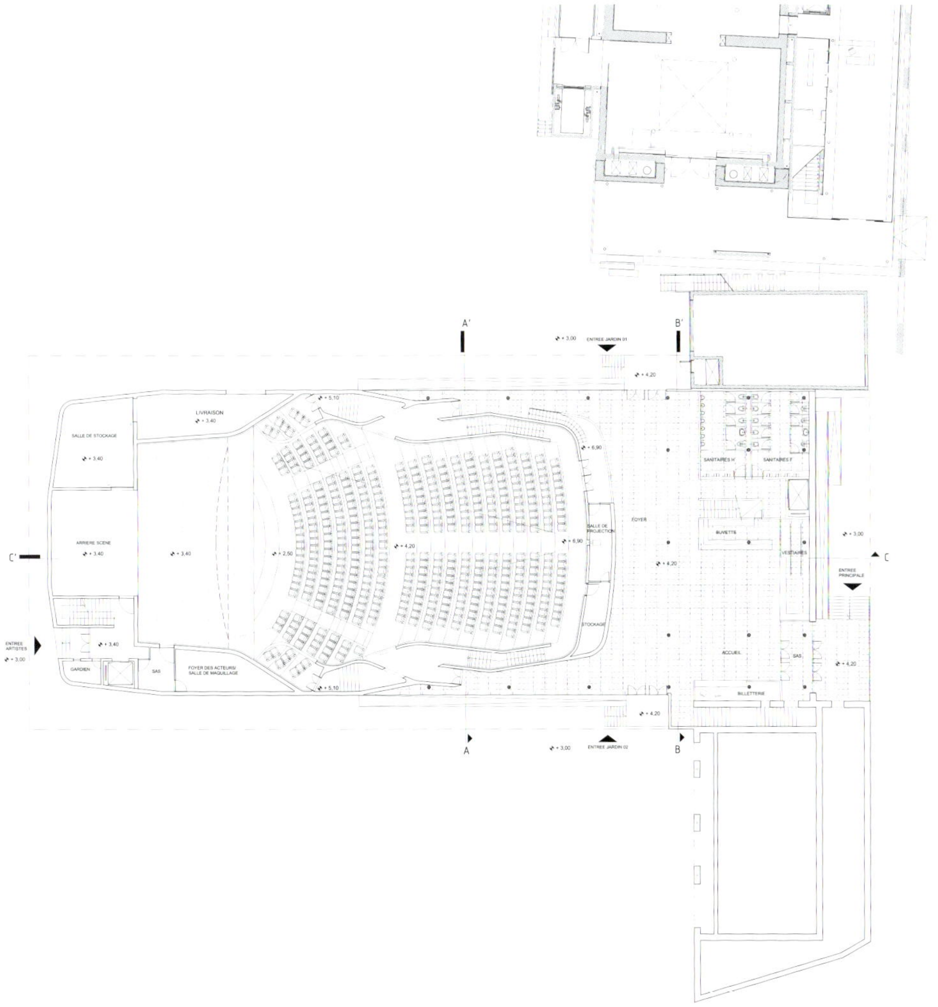

← | **Ground floor plan**
↓ | **Auditorium** with different seating zones, wood cladding and optimized ceiling structure

5+1AA / Alfonso Femia, Gianluca Peluffo

↑ | **Main entrance**
↓ | **Section**

New Cinema Palace

Venice

The design of the new Cinema Palace of Venice is part of the Congress Center redevelopment and may be seen as an approach to cope with the fantastic and magical character of movies themselves. It is a magical box, hiding its secret from the outside world while acting as a barrier between the exterior's realism and the fascinating atmosphere inside. The huge body of the building seems to rise from the ground level as a soft hill and opens itself to the outside only on one front via a mosaic glass façade. Inside the building, spacious foyers and halls executed in delicate materials awaken the visitor's impressions of being a part of a movie.

PROJECT FACTS

Address: Lido di Venezia, Venice, Italy. **Interior Design:** 5+1AA & Rudy Ricciotti. **Client:** Municipality of Venice. **Completion:** 2011. **Number of seats:** all audiences: 3310; main audience: 2400. **Main materials:** sound-proofing moquette, resin. **Setting:** urban.

↑ | **The Cinema Square**

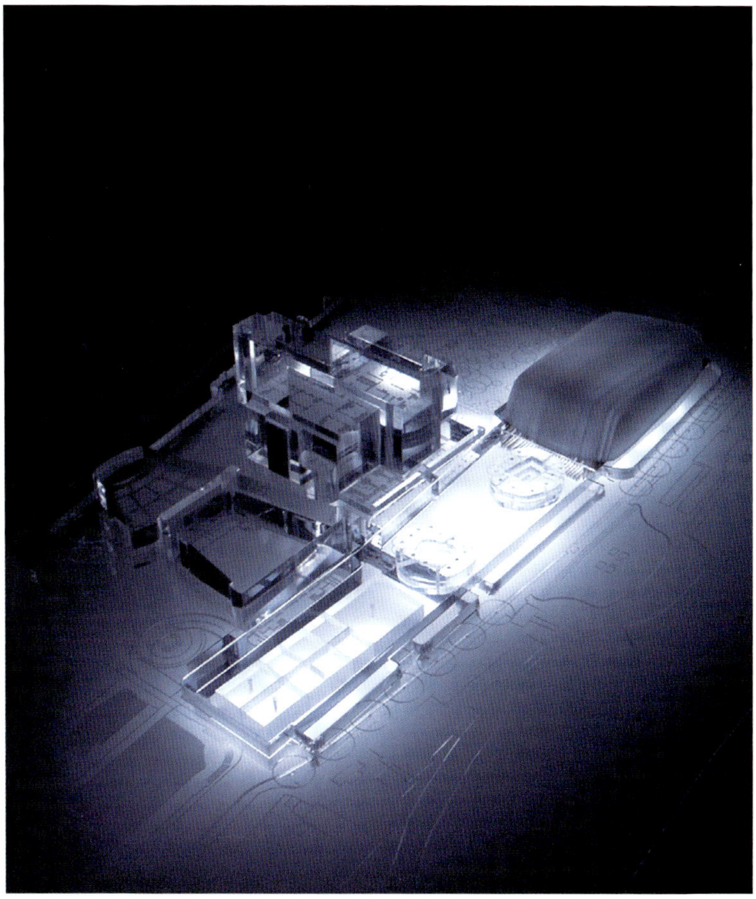

↑ | **Aerial view,** the Cinema Palace is part of the Congress Center

↓ | **Interior view,** hallway with mosaic glass façade

Soeters Van Eldonk architecten

↑ | **View of façade on street side** with gateway to Mariënburgplein
→ | **Red brick façade**, view from square

Lux

Nijmegen

The gate building, housing a partially sunken theater and cinema, forms the spatial end of the elevated Mariënburgplein. The shrunken public space is the theme here: the Mariënburg Chapel is hemmed in by the building, resembling a big elephant in too small an enclosure. Two differently designed façades are to be found on either side, referring to the theater and cinema auditoriums. The theater façade facing the square was designed as a red curtain with white ornaments and ruffles on the bottom. On the street side, it is defined by the five cinema auditoria, which are identifiable as separate volumes in the façade. Visitors can access the building via the entrance in the covered gateway. The interior is dominated by a Giovanni Battista Piranesi-like ambience.

PROJECT FACTS

Address: Mariënburg 38–39, 6511 PS Nijmegen, The Netherlands. **Client:** VOF Mariënburg: City Council of Nijmegen, ING Realestate. **Completion:** 2000. **Number of seats:** 504. **Largest screen diameter:** 11.37 m. **Sound equipment:** Dolby Digital. **Kind of projection:** 35 mm, 16 mm, HD, videobeam. **Additional functions:** café/restaurant, theater, concert hall, debate hall. **Main materials:** exterior: brick; interior: concrete. **Setting:** inner city.

←←| **Interior view,** foyer and staircase
← | **Section**
↓ | **Interior view,** restaurant

OMA – Office for Metropolitan Architecture with Prada / Rem Koolhaas

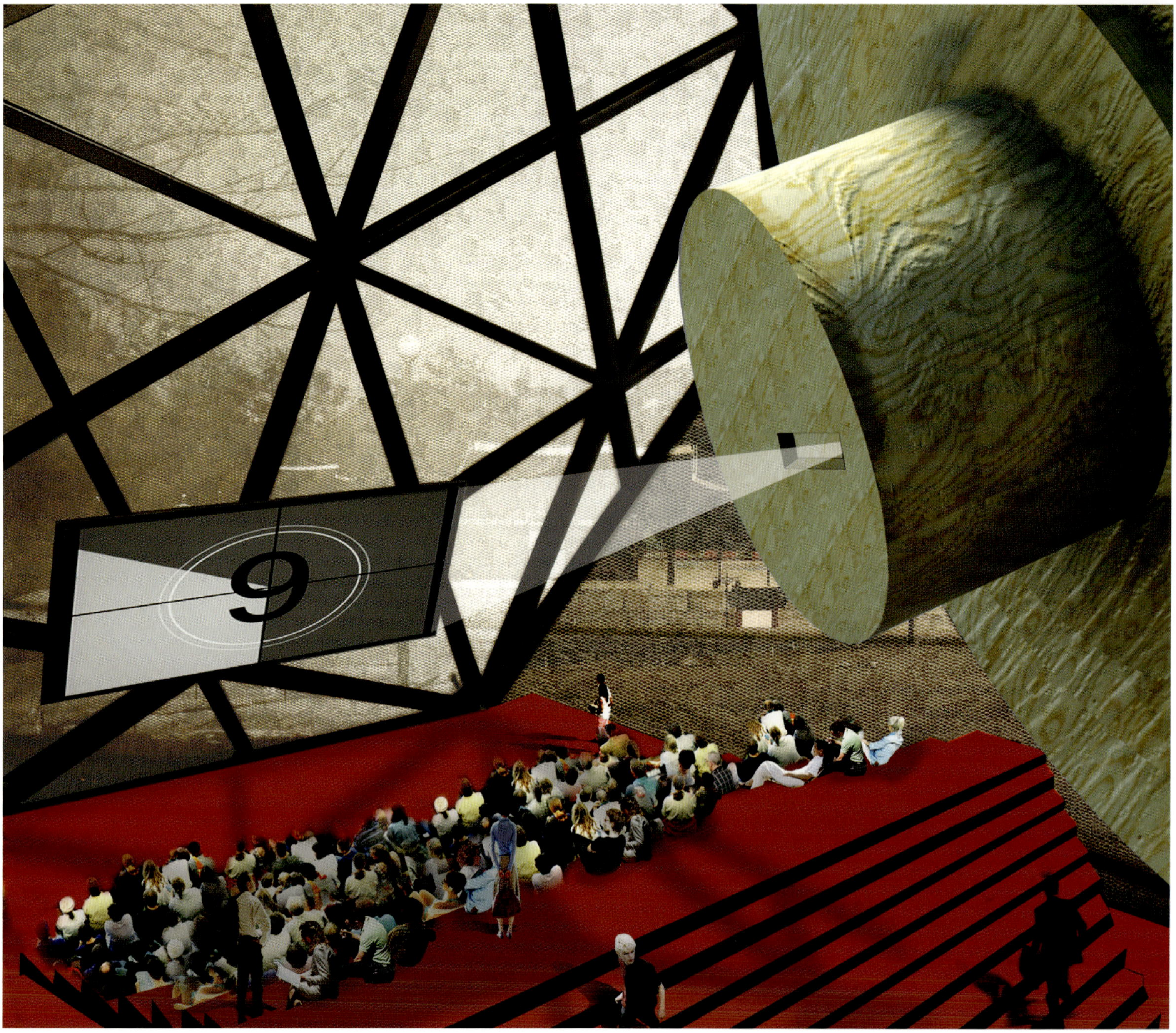

↑ | **Interior view,** cinema use

Prada Transformer

anywhere

The Transformer is a mobile architectural concept for the Prada Group, which can be adjusted to various uses. Primarily an exhibition hall, it can also be used for presentations, including a catwalk, a frontal stage or movie screenings. Depending on the use, a different side of the construction serves as the floor, while cranes turn the 80 tons of membrane-covered steel into the right position. For exhibitions, the cross-shaped frame construction serves as the floor, the hexagonal side is used for fashion shows, the rectangular side for cinematography, and the round side is used for special events. The cylinder at the center of this side serves as a technical room and is the projection room for movies.

PROJECT FACTS

Address: anywhere. **Client:** Prada. **Completion:** 2009. **Number of seats:** 100. **Largest screen diameter:** 8 m. **Sound equipment:** Dolby surround; 5 channels. **Kind of projection:** Barko Digital cinema projectors, 2x 18,000 lumen. **Additional functions:** event center. **Main materials:** steel, membrane. **Setting:** anywhere.

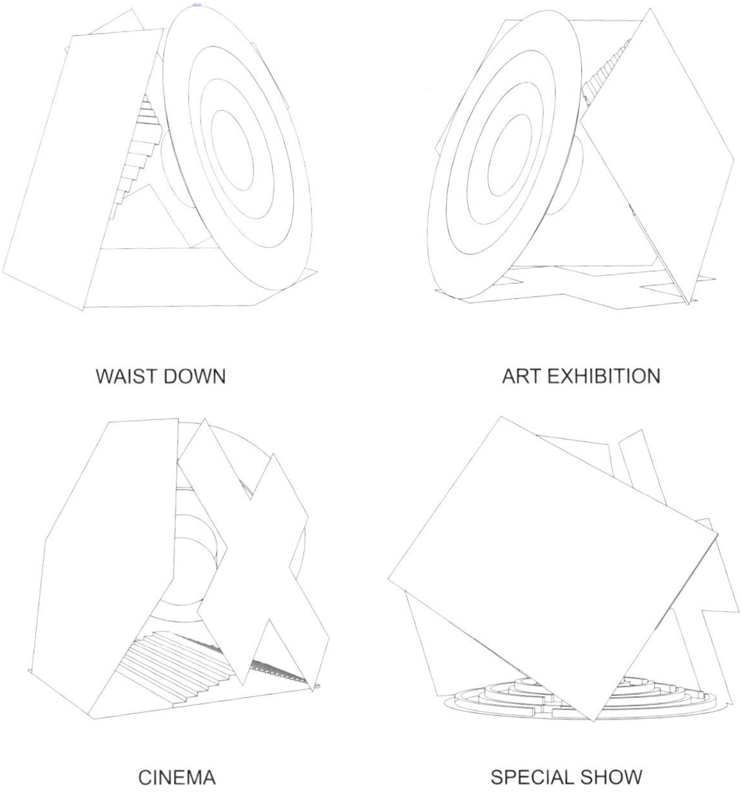

↑ | **Geometries,** four different functions
↓ | **Exterior**

↑ | **Art exhibition,** waist down – skirts by Miuccia Prada

Muungano

↑ | **Library bus,** richly decorated by Frederik Forsberg
↗ | **Couch for watching movies**
→ | **Interior with bookshelves**

Bookbus

Kiruna

The function of this media vehicle is to supply a larger service, where new digital media, as well as traditional printed material, are presented side by side. In addition to distributing media, the bus will also function as a place for people to communicate on the web and enable meetings between different groups. The layout is designed to maximize offered services and media. The front is organized like a traditional library with many bookshelves and stools. The back caters to a younger audience and includes music, film and computer media. This section may also be used for lectures and film screenings. In order to optimally use the limited space, the movie screen can be lowered whenever a screening is to take place.

PROJECT FACTS

Address: around the city of Kiruna, Sweden. **Interior Design:** Muungano / Martin Hedenström and Peter Thuvander. **Exterior graphics:** Fredrik Forsberg. **Client:** Kiruna City Library. **Completion:** 2008. **Number of seats:** 10–15. **Additional functions:** library. **Main materials:** exterior: steel; interior: textile seating, rubber floor. **Setting:** mobile.

↑ | Library bus at night

← | Plan and sections

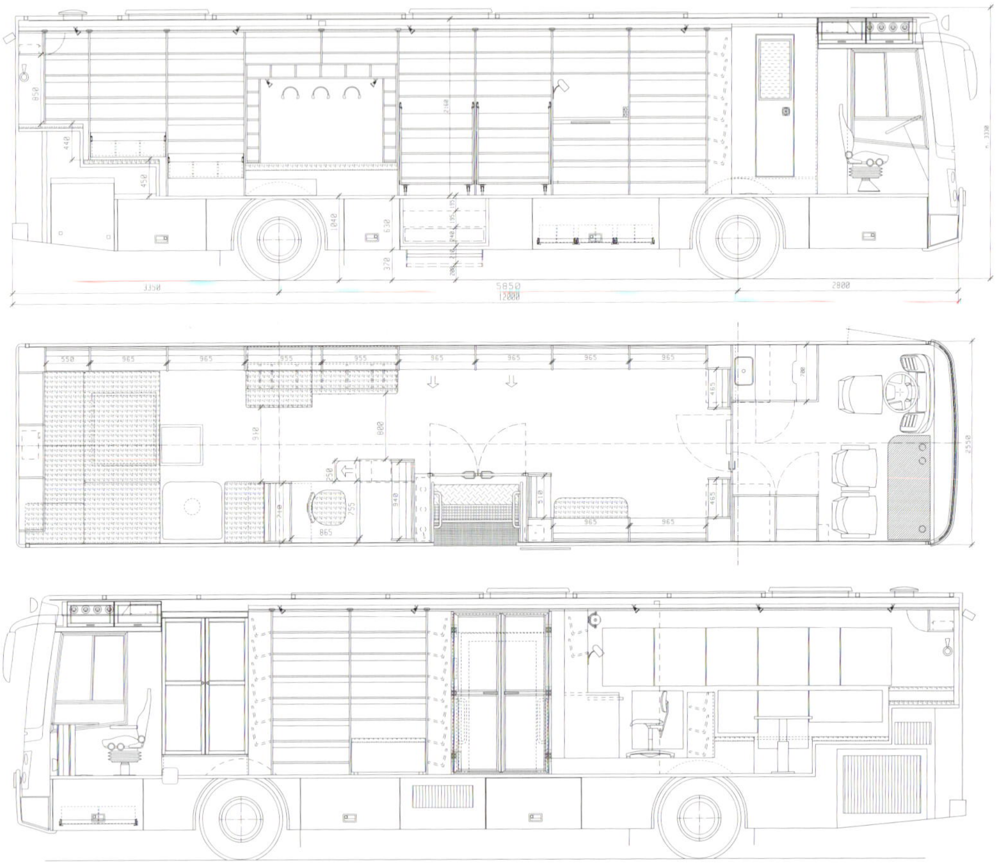

← | **Bookshelves and audio facilities**
↓ | **Exterior with graphics,** by Frederik Forsberg

Rojkind Arquitectos /
Michel Rojkind

↑ | **Exterior view** by day
→ | **Plaza** by night

Cultural and Educational Center

Kuwait

The concept for the Educational and Cultural Center rings in a new architectural era for the city of Kuwait. It simultaneously provides a new city-wide landmark and skyline, and crafts an intimate integration of public and private spaces within the city. The complex contains an extensive amount of spaces divided into three main zones, each with a unique set of requirements and relationships. The different zones are positioned a dozen meters above ground level allowing for extensive public spaces like plazas and shaded walkways below. The cinema is housed in the third Performance and Design zone along with other facilities like theaters and concert halls.

PROJECT FACTS

Address: Kuwait, United Emirates. **Structural engineer:** Ove Arup & Partners. **Client:** confidential. **Completion:** 2006. **Number of seats:** all audiences: 2,091; main audience: 561. **Largest screen diameter:** 22.5 m. **Sound equipment:** Dolby CP650 Digital Processors. **Kind of projection:** Digital Projection DCI Compliant. **Additional functions:** museum, exhibition center, public library, conference center, music center, theater, office, commercial space. **Main materials:** concrete. **Setting:** urban.

↑ | Interior view

← | Second floor plan

← | Section
↓ | Interior view

architectenbureau Fritz

↑ | **Interior view,** bar and balcony within the large auditorium
→ | **Exterior view** from Willemsplein

Luxor

Arnhem

In 1915, Luxor was the preeminent movie theater boasting premier technology. This was also visually communicated by featuring a variety of luscious architectural styles on its façade. In 2008, Luxor was converted to a contemporary multi-use center. However, the original elements of interior design and architecture were restored or reconstructed. New spaces and elements (balcony, basement, elevator) were added, others replaced (LEDs). The expanded function effected the building's physics and technology: noise insulation, light and sound system, infrastructure for food and drink services were successfully integrated while continuing to use old infrastructure. The building's second skin houses air conditioning technology and helps maintain strict environmental and noise regulations.

PROJECT FACTS

Address: Willemsplein 10, 6811 KB Arnhem, The Netherlands. **Planning partner:** Municipality of Arnhem. **Client:** Municipality of Arnhem. **Completion:** 2008. **Number of seats:** all audiences: 272; main audience: 202. **Largest screen diameter:** 5.66 m. **Sound equipment:** Electro Voice (PIEEE). **Kind of projection:** Beamer and LCD screens. **Additional functions:** pop podium, theater, café. **Main materials:** exterior: brick, steel, natural stone; interior: wood, plaster, steel, terrazzo. **Setting:** inner city.

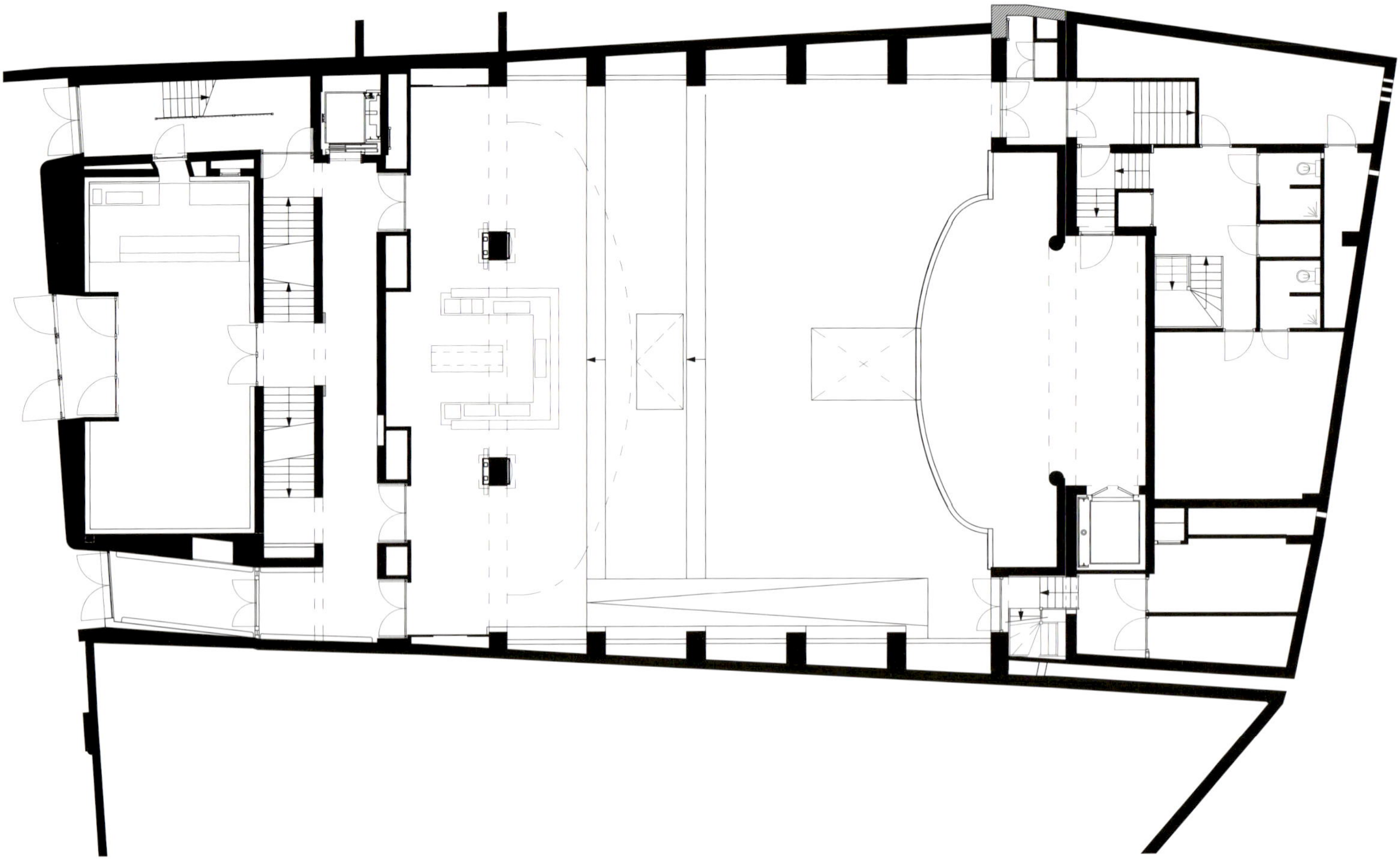

↑ | **Ground floor plan**
← | **Detail,** ornaments on a pillar

← | **Staircase**

↓ | **Stage and bar** of the small auditorium

Riepl Riepl Architekten /
Peter Riepl, Gabriele Riepl

↑ | **Entrance**
↗ | **Mezzanine floor**
→ | **Foyer,** first floor

Kulturhaus Römerfeld / Landesmusikschule Windischgarsten

Windischgarsten

The new building's longitudinal stretch highlights the physical conclusion of the edge of the compact village structure at the transition to its peripheral areas. The loosened horizontal layering and the large openings convey the building's interior openness while underlining the inviting character of the building. The key components such as music school, hall and dining are clearly distinguishable as individual building modules, yet constitute a single coherent structure. The music school is accessible via a glazed atrium, which vividly represents the complex interaction of exterior and interior spaces, the theme of the entire building.

PROJECT FACTS

Address: Gleinkerseestraße 13, 4580 Windischgarsten, Austria. **Light Design:** Brigitte Kowanz. **Structuralt engineers:** Kirsch Muchitsch & Partner. **Client:** Marktgemeinde Windischgarsten. **Completion:** 2004. **Number of seats:** 500. **Largest screen diameter:** 6.52 m. **Sound equipment:** Martin Audio. **Additional functions:** auditorium, music school, gastronomy. **Main materials:** exterior: precast concrete, glass; interior: concrete, stucco, unplastered plasterboard. **Setting:** rural.

↑ | Audience
← | Gallery

← | **Foyer,** first floor
↓ | **Section**
↓↓ | **Ground floor plan**

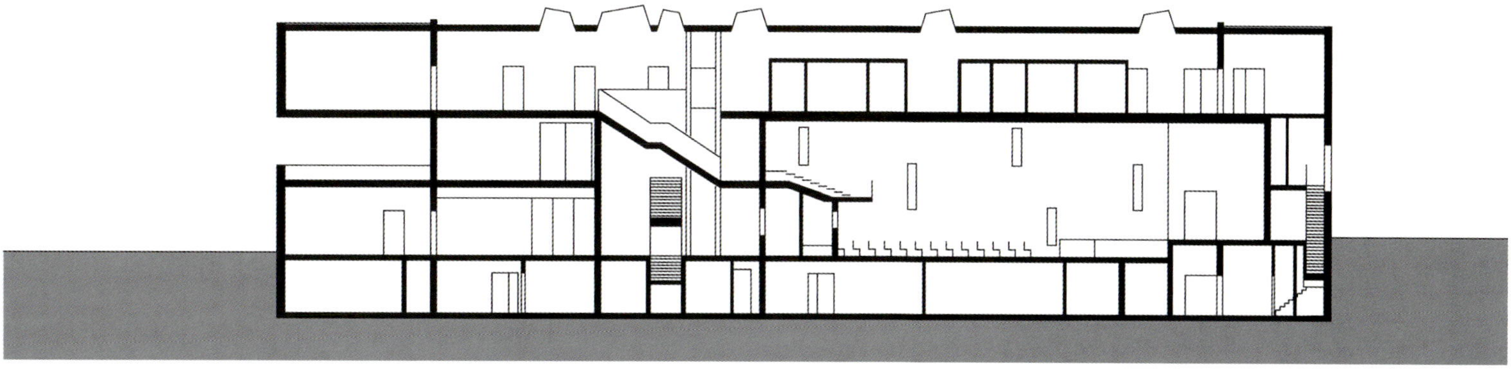

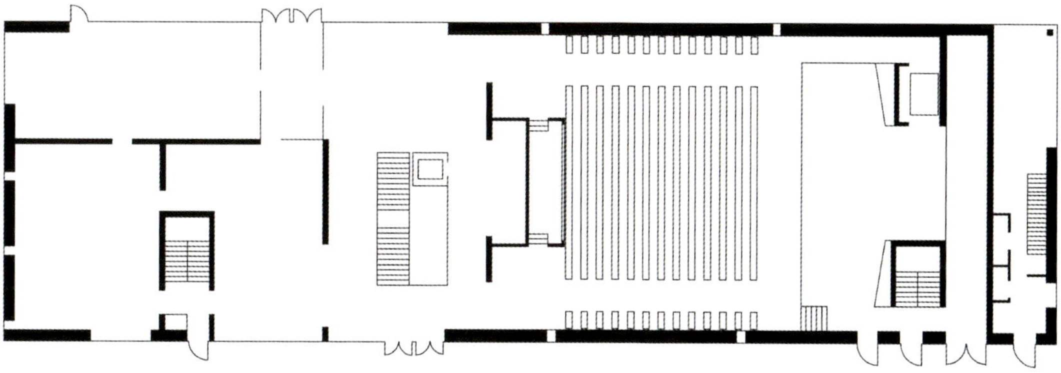

Atelier Aires Mateus /
Manuel Aires Mateus,
Francisco Aires Mateus

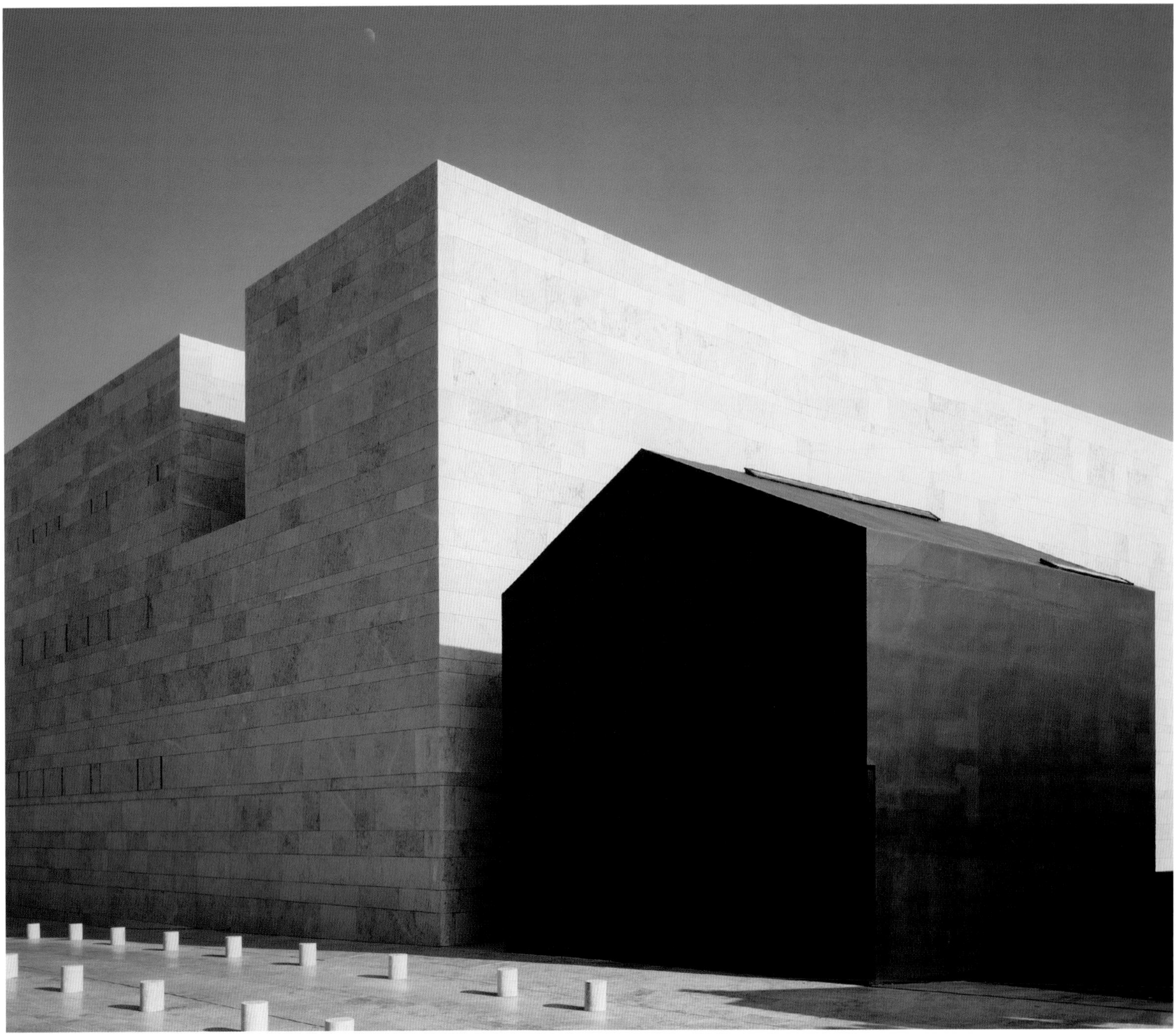

↑ | Exterior view
→ | Perspective

Centro de Artes de Sines

Sines

The building is situated at the start of the main street which links the town to the sea and marks the traditional entrance to the historic center. Diverse activities, capable of generating an exceptional array of services, are combined in the building: exhibition rooms, a library, cinema-cum-theater and a documentation center. The wide-ranging program calls for the whole plot to be occupied, enveloping the street below the main ground level and adapting its exterior volume to the monumental scale of the adjacent castle walls. The four modules have decks hung from a bridge-like structure which guarantees a continuous view across the building's interior, including the Center's activities in relation to the daily life of the town.

PROJECT FACTS

Address: Rua Cândido dos Reis, 7520 Sines, Portugal. **Structural Engineer:** Miguel Vilar - BETAR. **Electrical Engineer:** Raul Serafim. **Client:** Câmara Municipal de Sines. **Completion:** 2005. **Setting:** urban.

↖ | **Interior view,** corridor
↑ | **Interior view,** stair case
← | **Perspective**

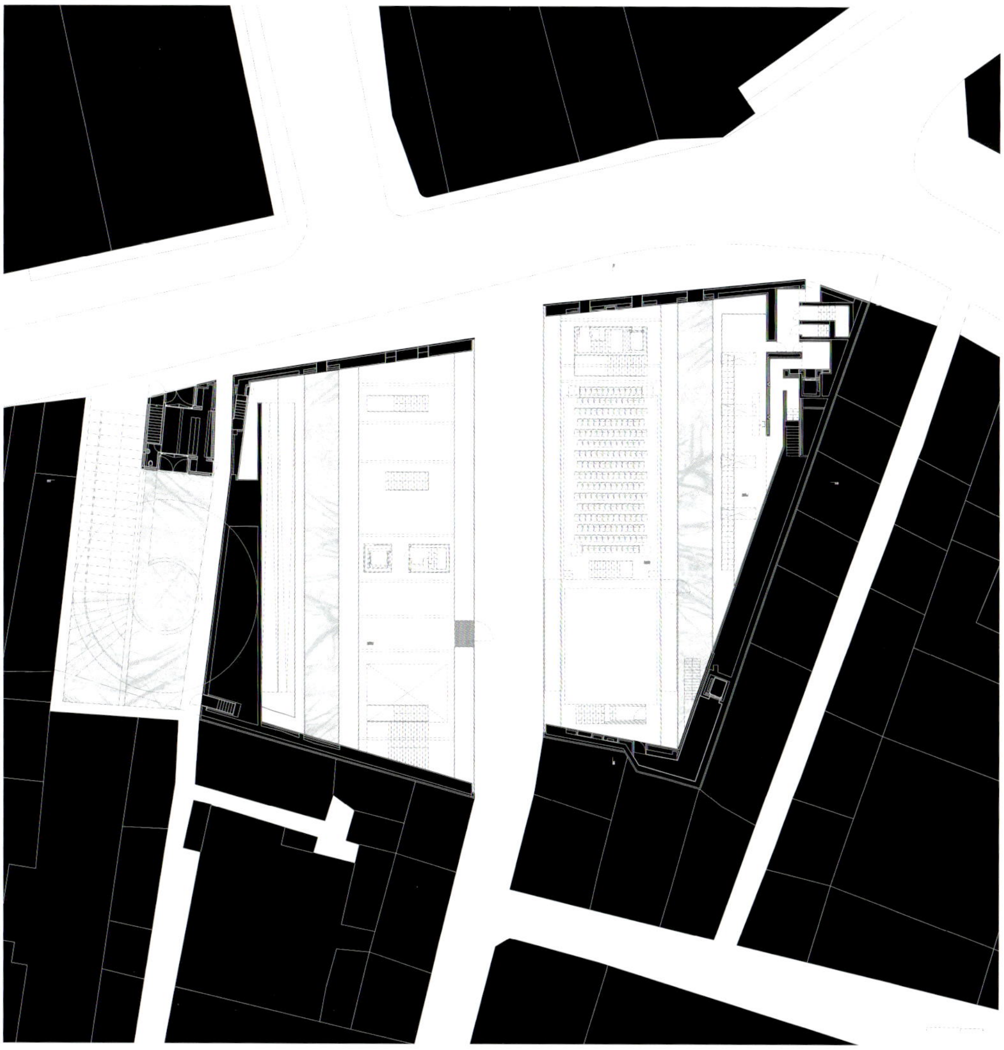

← | **Ground floor plan** with auditorium
↓ | **View** through the window to the old town of Sines

Henket & partners architecten

↑ | **Exterior view,** new extension
↓ | **Different sections**

Verkadefabriek

's-Hertogenbosch

The Centre for Performing Arts De Verkadefabriek symbolizes the blurring of the boundaries between different art forms, and brings performances, debates and meetings together under one roof. The center offers accommodations for three theatrical companies with its theater auditoria (250- and 150-seat capacity) and rehearsal rooms; an art house cinema (150-, 75- and 50-seat capacity); a theater café and offices. A major goal of the project was to preserve the utilitarian character of the former waffle factory which resonates throughout the design of the new development. The complex is located within a stone's throw from the historic town center and the main station. In terms of its concept and size, the Verkade factory surpasses similar initiatives.

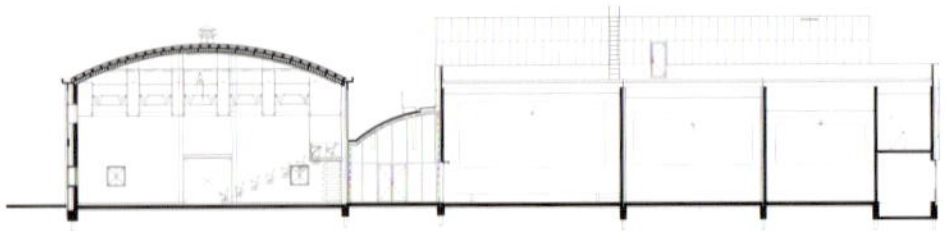

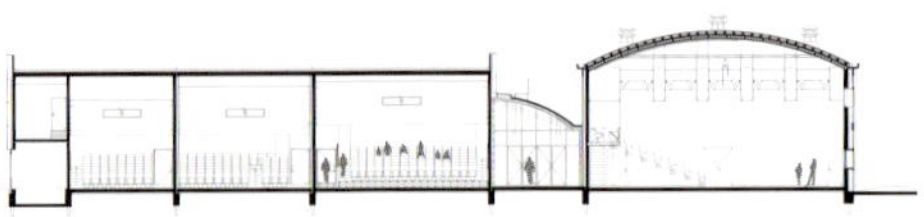

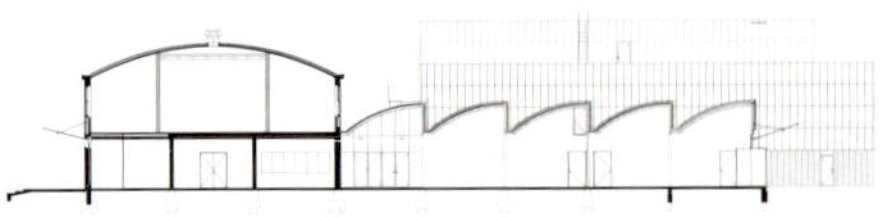

PROJECT FACTS

Address: Verkadefabriek, Boschdijkstraat 45, 5211 VD 's-Hertogenbosch, The Netherlands. **Planning partner:** D3BN civiel ingenieurs, Huisman & Van Muijen, Adviesbureau Peutz en Associés, Bremen Bouwadviseurs, Piet Hein Eek (interior café/restaurant), MTD Landschapsarchitecten. **Client:** Municipality s-Hertogenbosch. **Completion:** 2004. **Number of seats:** all audiences: 275; main audience: 150. **Additional functions:** restaurant, rehearsal rooms, offices. **Setting:** inner city.

↑ | **Interior view,** café of the theater
↓ | **Theater auditorium**

↑ | **Auditorium,** dominated by the color purple

3D IMAX Science Museum

London

Like a giant spaceship, the 450-seat IMAX cinema enigmatically floats in the generous volume of the Science Museum's Welcome Wing designed by MacCormac Jamieson Prichard. In addition to showing 2D and 3D scientific films and acting as a science lectures venue, it helps to move visitors to the museum's upper levels. The auditorium is suspended three storys above and is enclosed by a perforated, curving underbelly, through which visitors are transported via a long escalator. Upon entering, they face a lighting installation developed specifically for the scheme: dichroic glass filters and emulsion paint create a spectrum of light in which colors overlap to create a pattern of movement.

PROJECT FACTS

Address: Exhibition Road, London, SW7 2DD, United Kingdom. **Client:** The National Museum of Science and Industry. **Completion:** 2001. **Number of seats:** 450. **Largest screen diameter:** 16.3 m. **Sound equipment:** Dolby sound system. **Kind of projection:** 2D and 3D IMAX projection. **Additional functions:** part of the National Museum of Science and Industry. **Main materials:** exterior: suspended perforated curving metal panels; interior: painted plasterboard. **Setting:** urban.

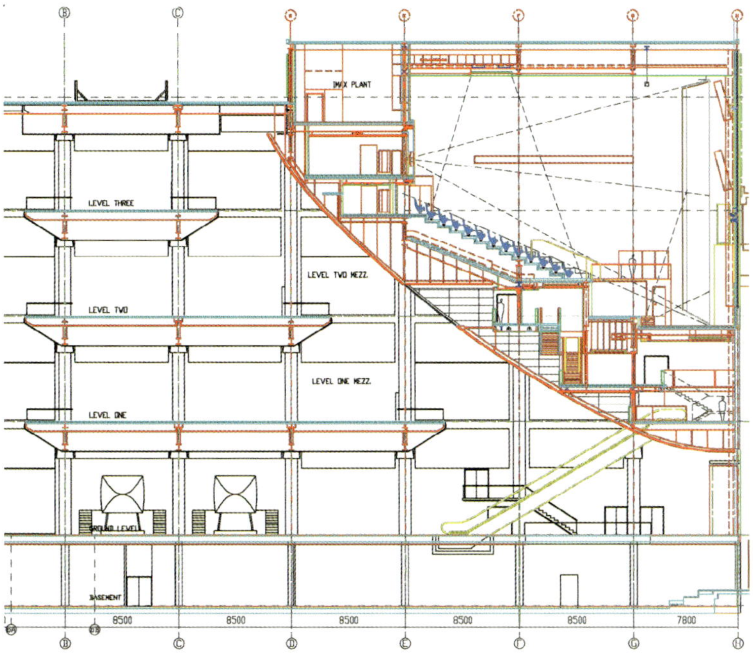

↑ | **Section** through auditorium showing construction
↓ | **Interior view,** underbelly of the auditorium

↑ | **Escalator,** access to the auditorium

Detlev Schneider

↑ | **CineCittá,** by night

CineCittá and IMAX Cinema

Nuremberg

CineCittá multiplex cinema, Germany's largest cinema complex, is located in the heart of Nuremberg's old town. By incorporating building structures with various shapes and sizes, the complex fits into the urban structure. The 21 movie theaters, Europe's largest IMAX cinema with a 1,000 square meter-cupola screen, and MAD simulation cinema with seats that move hydraulically in sync with the movie, plus 4,000 square meter of lobby space constitute an extensive activity and event area. In the lobby area, 13 bars and three restaurants offer a wide range of extended leisure activities. Beyond Nuremberg, the CineCittá is also renown for offering "alternative content", especially opera live transmissions with up to 1,200 visitors.

PROJECT FACTS

Address: Gewerbemuseumsplatz 3, 90403 Nuremberg, Germany. **Client:** Wolfram Weber. **Completion:** 1997. **Number of seats:** 5,000. **Largest screen diameter:** 37 m; cupola IMAX cinema: 30 m. **Sound equipment:** D-Cinema Sound 5.1. (CineCittá), Sonics Sound-System (IMAX Sound). **Kind of projection:** Christie Digital Systems, 35 mm Kinoton DP30. **Additional functions:** theater, café, bar, restaurants. **Main materials:** concrete, aluminum. **Setting:** inner city.

↑ | **Interior,** CineCittá

↑ | **IMAX cinema** with cupola

↓ | **Site plan**

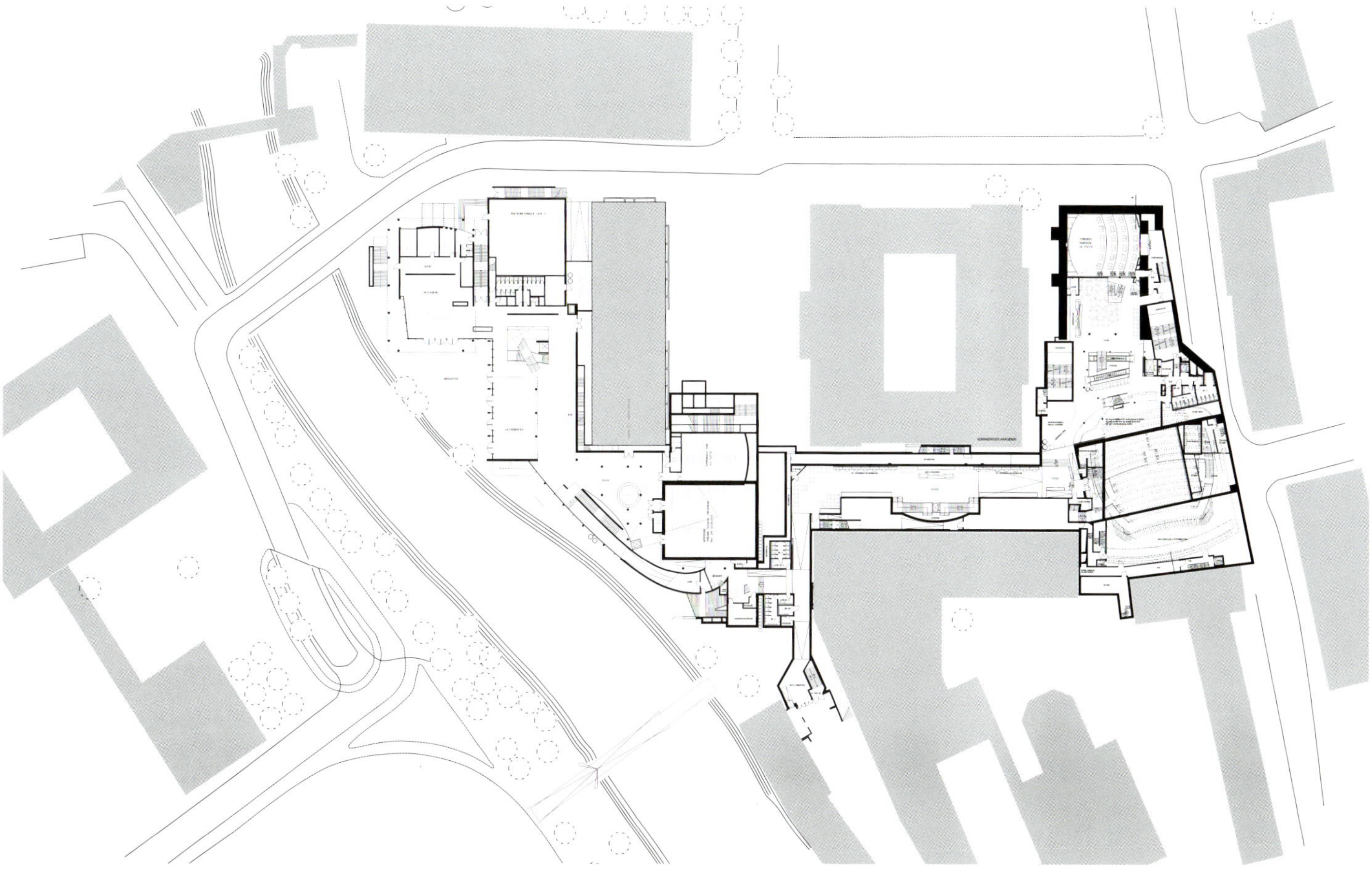

↑ | Cinema 1

Arsenal Cinema Sony Center

Berlin

Filmhaus Berlin is located inside the Sony Center on Potsdamer Square, built according to plans by Murphy/Jahn Architects, Chicago, and completed in 2000. The final construction of the German Cinematheque - Film and Television Museum (design by Hans-Dieter Schaal), Arsenal Cinema and dffb (German Film and Television Academy) was executed by Lehrecke Architects, Berlin. The wide range of cinema viewings offered by Arsenal Cinema of international film weeks (silent films, conferences, experimental cinema, etc.) is presented to the public in the larger theater (230 seats) and a small studio (75 seats). Both cinemas have custom-designed rows of folding seats with wool or leather upholstery.

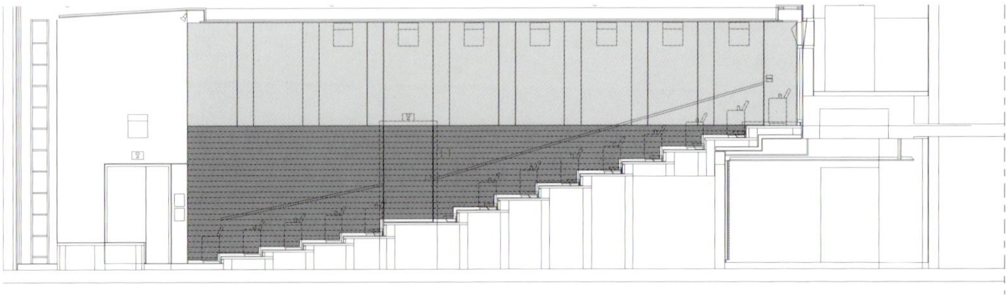

Address: Potsdamer Straße 2, 10787 Berlin, Germany. **Architect Sony Center:** Murphy/Jahn Architects Chicago. **Client:** City of Berlin, Kulturverwaltung. **Completion:** 2000. **Number of seats:** 311. **Largest screen diameter:** 9.84 m. **Sound equipment:** JBL. **Kind of projection:** 35 mm and 70 mm Kinoton FP 75E, 16 mm FP 18E. **Additional functions:** museum, library, Deutsche Kinemathek, Deutsche Film- und Fernseh-akademie. **Main materials:** exterior: glass, steel; interior: aluminum, wood, fabric. **Setting:** inner city.

↑ | **Cinema 2**
↙ | **Section,** cinema 1

↓ | **Sony Center,** cupola

↑ | Foyer
↓ | Second floor plan

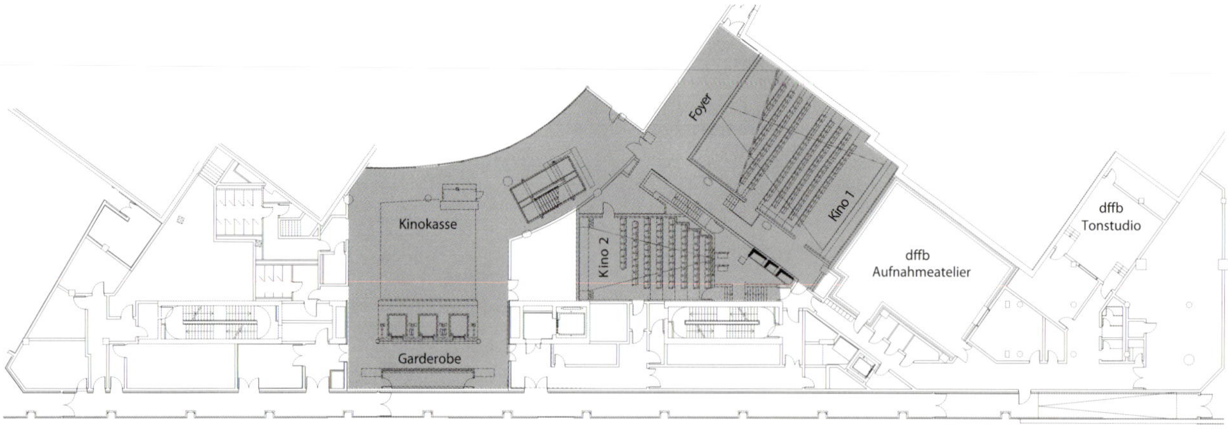

← | **Entrance**, cinema 1
↙ | **Corridor**
↓ | **Perspective**, cinema 1

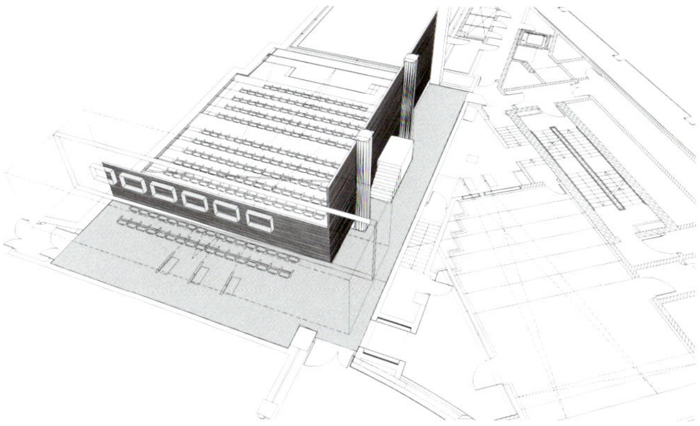

Wallrath & Weinert Architekten

↑ | **View from street side**
→ | **Inner courtyard,** main entrance

Cinema and Culture Center

Kassel

This area close to the Documenta art exhibition location was originally organized into strict neo-classical blocks. The new cinema center sees itself as a connector of various city structures, and on the one hand forms a compliment to the historical city blocks, while on the other mediates the neighboring post-war architecture characterized by strong traffic and tall building slabs. The building embeds itself like a pillow and reacts to various neighboring situations, which differ on all sides. The cinema's jutting-out, dynamic body visualizes the urbanism and movement of the congested town. The building's base fills the rectangular city space. The glazed foyer lets the spherical form of the cinema, placed in the middle, appear to be floating.

Address: Karlsplatz 8, 34117 Kassel, Germany. **Client:** Olympic Filmtheaterbetrieb Heinz Riech OHG&Sohn Dusseldorf – DEGI Frankfurt. **Completion:** 2000. **Number of seats:** all audiences: 3,400; main audience: 600. **Largest screen diameter:** 24 m. **Sound equipment:** THX-standard. **Additional functions:** music academy, restaurants, residences, offices. **Main materials:** exterior: stainless steel panels with linen structure; interior: parquet floor, stone ware, glass. **Setting:** inner city.

↑ | **View from street side,** corner with entrance area

← | **Ground floor plan,** foyer

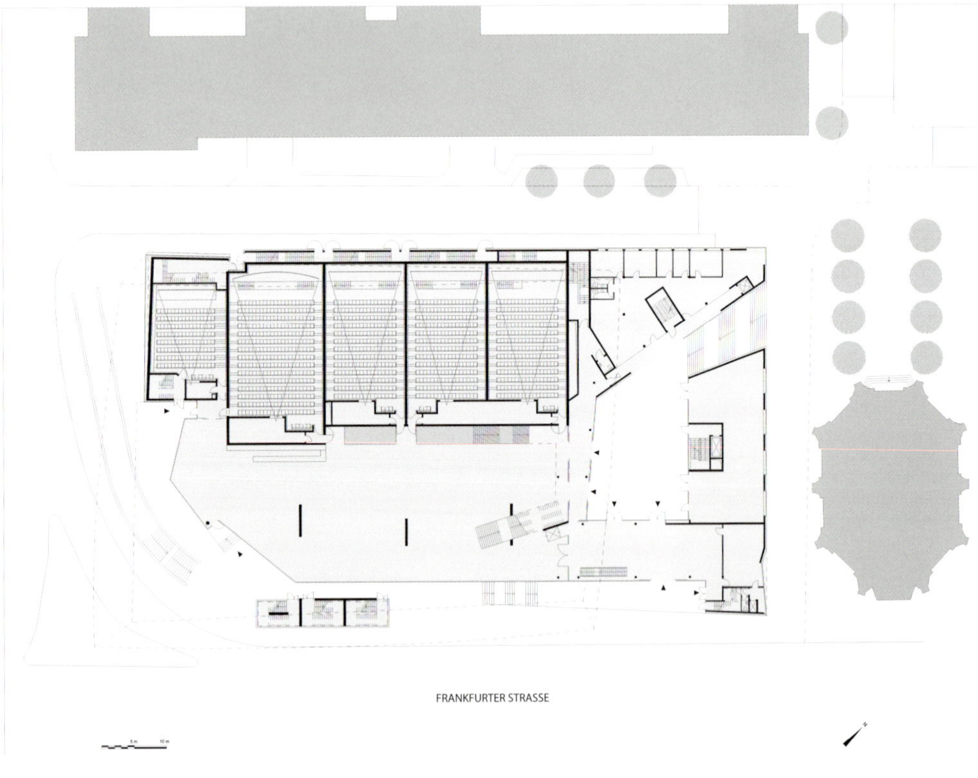

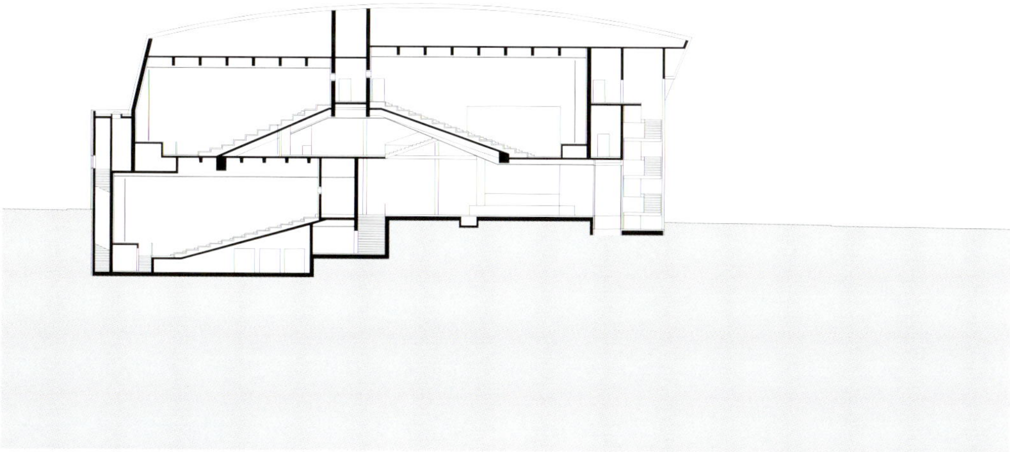

← | **Section**
↓ | **Music academy at the Karlsplatz** and staircase into the courtyard

Atelier de l'Île
(Dominique Brard Architecte)

↑ | **Audience 1**
→ | **Atrium** with information desk

Cinémathèque Française et Bibliothèque du film

Paris

The stone façade of the former American Center (1988–1994) was a novelty in Frank O. Gehry's work, referring to the traditional Parisian style. The monument remained unused for several years, but now houses the French national film center and a film library. The architects of Atelier de l'Île (Dominique Brard, Olivier Le Bras and Marc Quelen) remodeled the interior giving it a new identity while respecting Gehrys structure. Sven new sections had to be incorporated into the existing structure – four movie theaters, rooms for the permanent exhibition, and areas for temporary exhibits, a library with a media center, a museum shop, as well as administration and logistics. The complex shape of the building impeded with the homogeneity of the new additions.

Address: 51, rue de Bercy, rue de Pommard, 75012 Paris, France. **Client:** Ministère de la Culture et de la Communication, EMOC. **Completion:** 2005. **Original building:** allFrank O. Gehry, 1994. **Number of seats:** all audiences: 718; main audience: 415. **Main materials:** lime sandstone, Oregon-pine, galvanized steel. **Setting:** urban.

↖ | **Audience 1,** detail

↑ | **Exterior view,** entrance area from the park side

← | **Audience 1,** view to the screen

↓ | **Sketch**

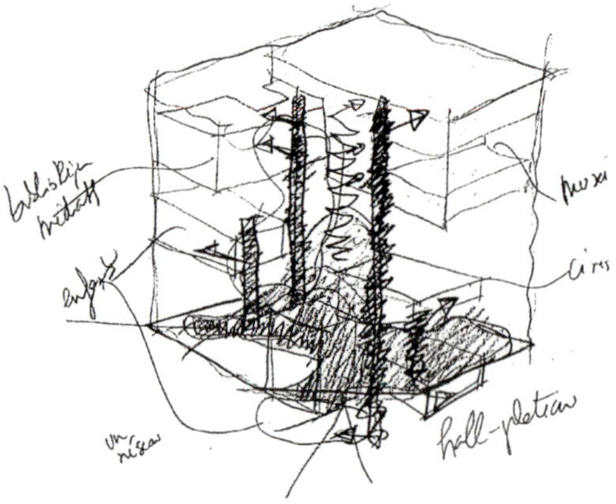

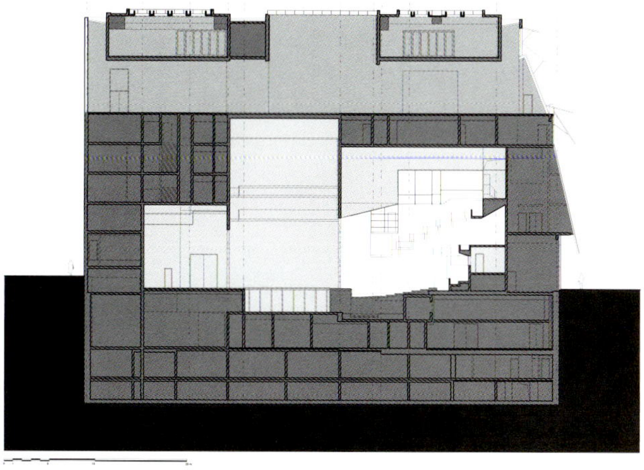

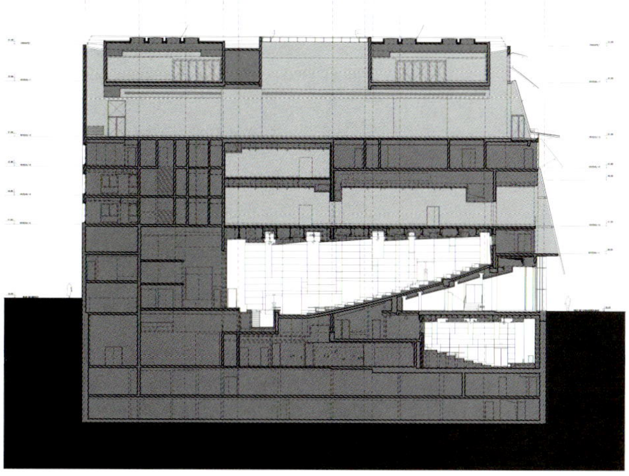

← | **Section,** before and after conversion
↓ | **New hall,** cinema cashpoint

Cust

omer-
focus

ATP Architekten und Ingenieure

↑ | **Audience,** warm colors create a cozy atmosphere
→ | **Cinema foyer**

CCL City Center Landshut

Landshut

Located in the Landshut city center, the shopping and amusement haven connects the historical downtown to the modern city pulse. On its five stories, the City Center Landshut offers high-quality shopping and entertainment along with more than 800 parking spaces. Fifty retail shops, food courts, as well as the 11-screen, 1,700-seat "Kinopolis" cinema occupy the center's 21,000 square meters. The highly modern, 455 square meter "SkyLight" event lounge in the Citydome offers a fascinating panorama view over the old town.

PROJECT FACTS

Address: Am Alten Viehmarkt 5, 84028 Landshut, Germany. **Planning partner:** Steidle + Partner. **Client:** CCL Entwicklungs GmbH. **Completion:** 2003. **Number of seats:** 1,700. **Setting:** inner city.

THE DAY AFTER TOMORROW
VAN HELSING

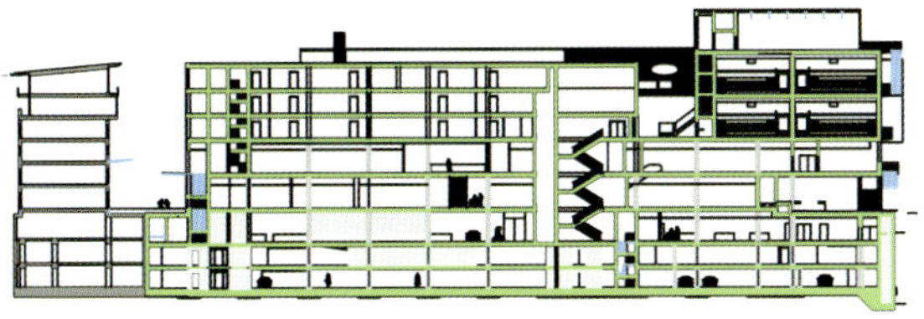

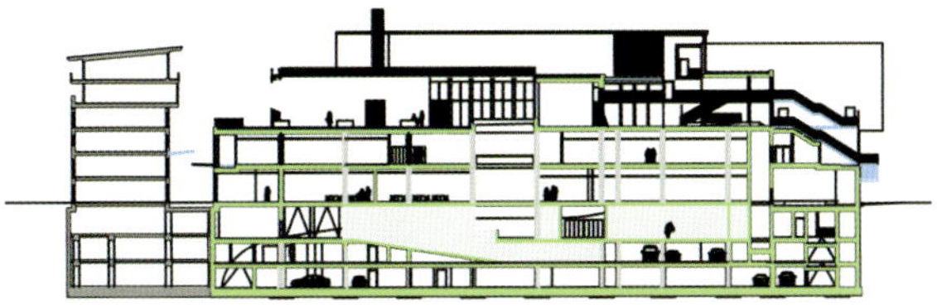

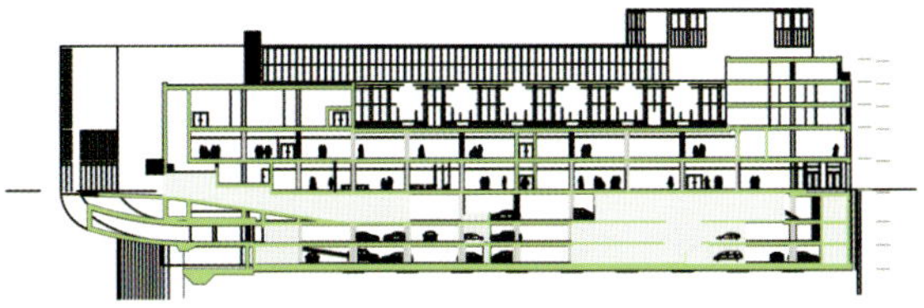

←←| **Façade Cinema center** by night
← | **Sections**
↓ | **Audience,** view to the seats and the projector

Arris Architects / Shubhashish Modi

↑ | **Main entrance**
→ | **Informal seating lounge** of stark white material

Fun Cinema

Lucknow

The Fun Cinema in Lucknow is part of the Fun Republic Mall, also designed by Arris Architects. The design approach followed the two main goals of creating a breathtaking atmosphere and optimally utilizing the limited space. A visual vortex came into being with the help of wood surfaces which were broken into facets. Each facet was carefully calculated for maximum space utilization. Complex geometry of surfaces in the hall, along with the material's warmth, result in a noble, comfortable as well as inspiring atmosphere serving as a kind of corridor between the real life of the mall and the fantastic world of the movies.

PROJECT FACTS

Address: Fun Republic Mall, Eldeco road, Lucknow, 226 010 Uttar Pradesh, India. **Planning partner:** Satish Shetty. **Interior Design:** Shubhashish Modi, Rohan Patil. **Client:** Fun Cinemas Pvt., Ltd. **Completion:** 2007. **Number of seats:** all audiences: 1,182; main audience: 358. **Largest screen diameter:** 16.78 m. **Sound equipment:** JBL. **Kind of projection:** Christie P-35. **Additional functions:** shopping mall, restaurants. **Main materials:** wood, Italian stone. **Setting:** urban.

↑ | **Corridor with seating zone** dominated by wooden veneer shell

← | **Stone seating ledge** below the skylight slit

← | View into one of the screens
↓ | Floor plan

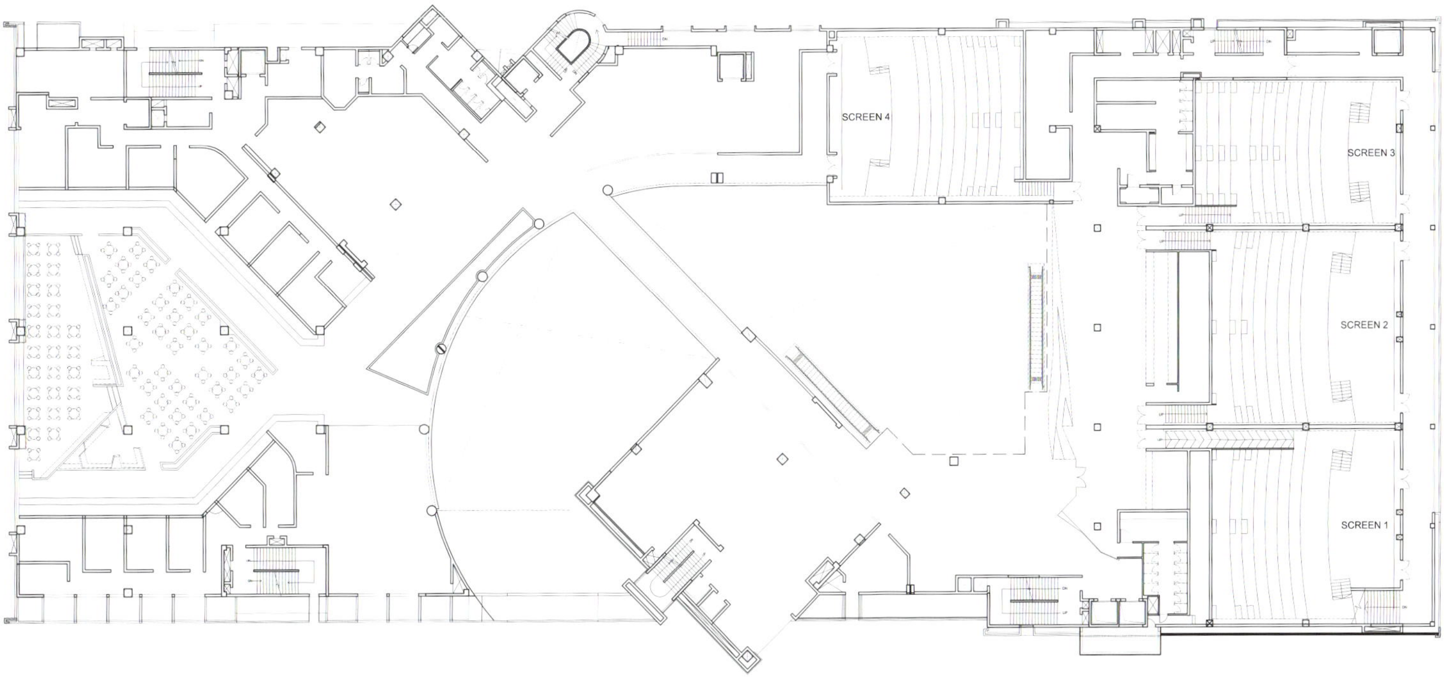

↑ | **Perspective,** plaza

La Cittadella

Kawasaki

La Cittadella, the new center of Kawasaki, Japan, is the first step in the process of rejuvenating the surrounding area. The site of the city's famous and newly relocated Club Citta, offers dining, shopping, cinema and nightclubs. La Cittadella will redefine the urban experience for residents and visitors. The site features a gently sloped circular path that carries visitors effortlessly from the street level past cafes, shops and restaurants to the upper-level entertainment and cinema area, which is one of the largest in the Tokyo metropolitan area. The layered design includes landscaped terraces, bridges and stepped gardens brimming with rich colors and textures.

PROJECT FACTS

Address: 4-1 Ogawacho, Kawasakiku, Kawasaki, Japan. **Client:** Citta Entertainment Co., Ltd. **Completion:** 2003. **Additional functions:** shopping center, dining/F&B, night club; open/public space, including 250-seat outdoor amphitheater. **Setting:** urban.

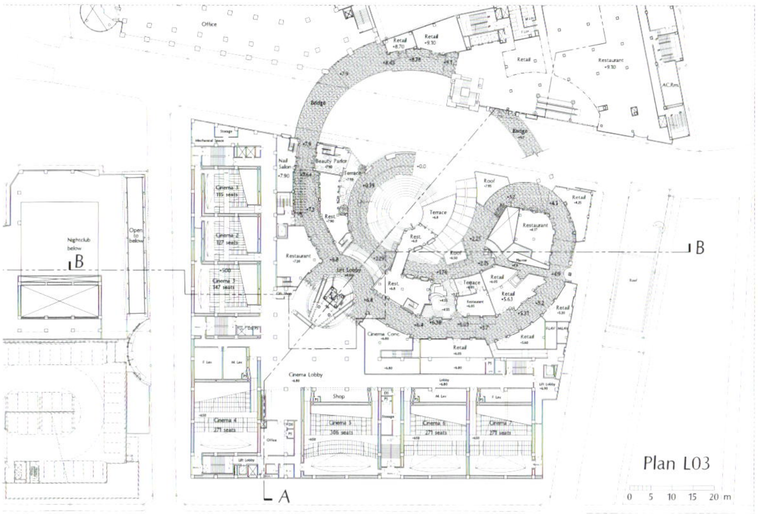

↑ | **Plan**
↓ | **Plaza by night**

↑ | **Different angles**

Arris Architects /
Satish Shetty

↑ | **Concession counter** wrapped in grey veneer envelope
→ | **Corridor**

Fun Cinema
Jaipur

The dynamic focal point of the entire design is visually evident in the gray veneered envelope which encompasses the concession counter and articulates it as the point of confluence and culmination for the spectators. The striking feature is a sense of motion created by the seemingly fluid orange wrap, discreetly used as the backdrop for the counter, and irregularly shaped seating. The use of light cove patterns accentuates the illusion of movement even further. Visually negotiating the clutter of structural elements and service technology was a challenge to resolve. Extensive use of red-colored back-painted glass and granite flooring visually reflects the warm ambience which became the identity associated with the space.

PROJECT FACTS

Address: Triton Mall, Jothara Road, Jaipur, Rajasthan, India. **Client:** Fun Multiplex Pvt., Ltd. **Completion:** 2009. **Number of seats:** all audiences: 958; main audience: 328. **Largest screen diameter:** 17.41 m. **Sound equipment:** JBL. **Kind of projection:** Christie CP-2K digital projector. **Additional functions:** shopping mall, restaurants. **Main materials:** duco lamination, granite. **Setting:** urban.

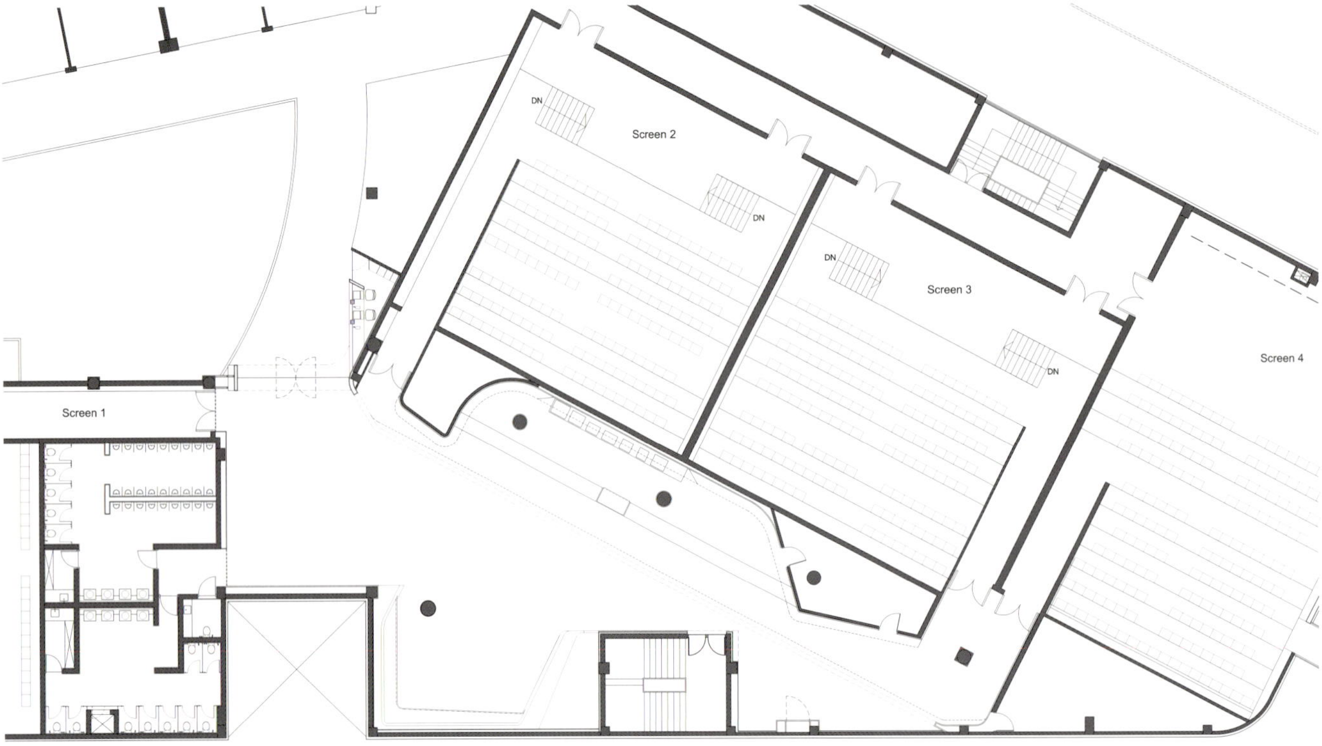

↑ | Floor plan
← | Inside one of the screens

← | **Color and light** playfully arranged in the corridor
↓ | **Concession counter**

Arris Architects / Satish Shetty

↑ | Entrance lobby
↗ | Opposite side of the lobby
→ | Seating area

Fun Cinema

Mumbai

The concessions for this cinema in Mumbai, the center of India's movie industry, are consciously crafted around the notion of materializing illusions. The attempt is made to amplify the experiences of these illusions by destabilizing the geometric form of a hexagon into a harmonious and functionally stable design which also accommodates the clients' functional requirements. The hexagonal partition acts as the focal point of the design, creating an ambience of a walk through an art exhibit. The location of recessed seating lobbies provides excellent vantage points for spectators, allowing them to appreciate the massive scale of the dynamic partition.

PROJECT FACTS

Address: K-Star Mall, Chembur, Mumbai, Maharashtra, India. **Planning partner:** Rohan Patil. **Client:** Fun Multiplex Pvt., Ltd. **Completion:** 2009. **Number of seats:** all audiences: 1,085; main audience: 282. **Largest screen diameter:** 13.6 m. **Sound equipment:** JBL. **Kind of projection:** Christie CP-2K digital projector. **Additional functions:** shopping mall, restaurants. **Main materials:** duco lamination, wood, Italian stone. **Setting:** urban.

↑ | Restroom

↙ | Floor plan

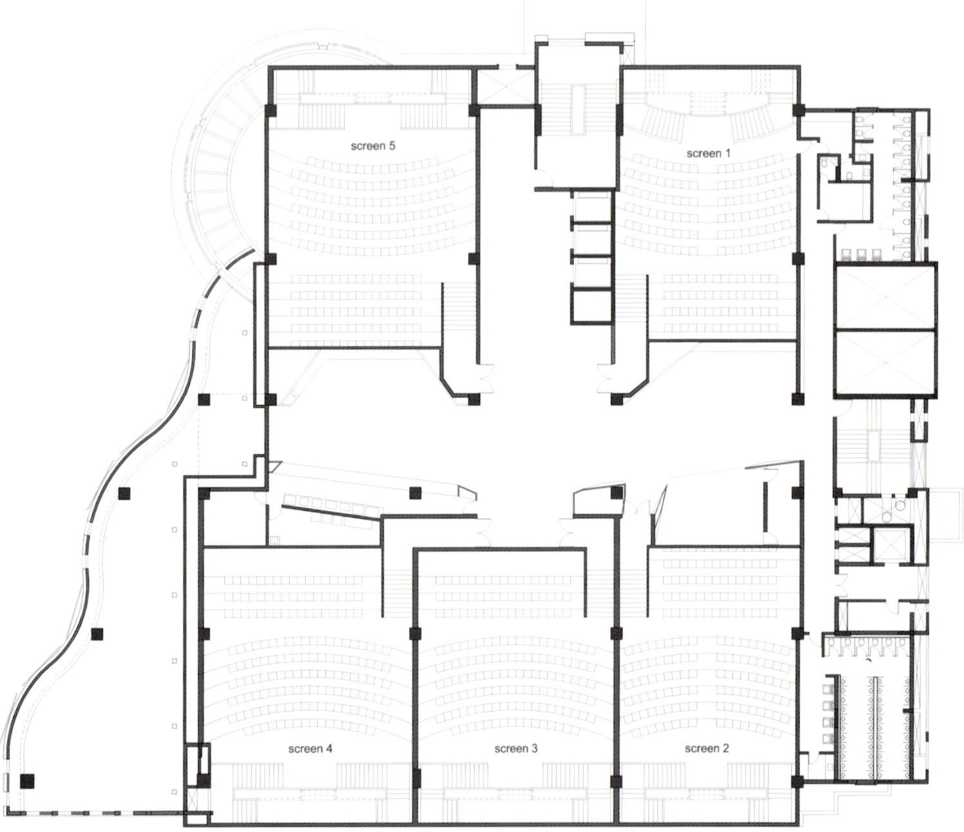

← | De-constructed hexagonal partition
↓ | Conceptual sketch

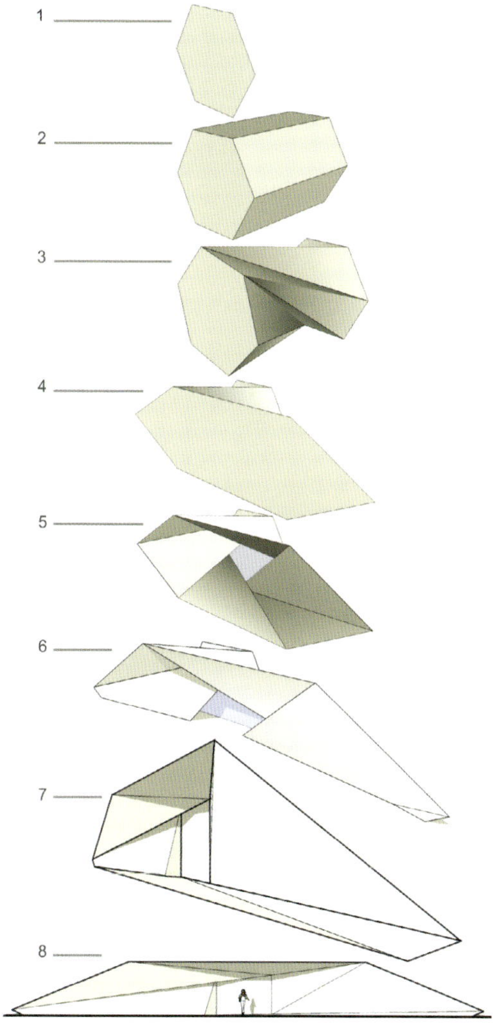

Kraaijvanger.Urbis / Rob Ligtvoet

↑ | **Front elevation cinema** with glass façade
→ | **Façade** of the office and apartment building

Het Turfschip

Breda

The redevelopment of the Turfschip area included the construction of a mega movie theater, a fitness center, offices and an underground parking garage. The area is conveniently located near the historic city center within easy reach of its commercial, cultural and recreational activities. The cinema foyer, with its glass drum-like façade, can be used as a giant projection screen. Seven theaters are housed in the building, serviced by one central control room. Both offices and apartments are located in the 12-story zinc clad building on the east side. The lower elongated building on the west side houses luxury apartments. The apartments and a low-rise housing block wrap around the cinema. The central axis leading towards the main entrance is accentuated by the pavement, which resembles a giant carpet.

Address: Chasséveld 15, 4811 DH Breda, The Netherlands. **Interior Design:** Concern. **Planning partner:** Goudstikker-de Vries (engineers). **Client:** Heijmans Vastgoed BV. **Completion:** 2008. **Number of seats:** all audiences: 1,396; main audience: 386. **Largest screen diameter:** 21,47 m. **Sound equipment:** Dolby Digital. **Kind of projection:** Cinemeccanica. **Additional functions:** apartments, offices, fitness center, gastronomy. **Main materials:** brick, zinc, glass, steel. **Setting:** inner city.

↑ | **Interior view,** glass front and seating area

← | **Third floor plan**

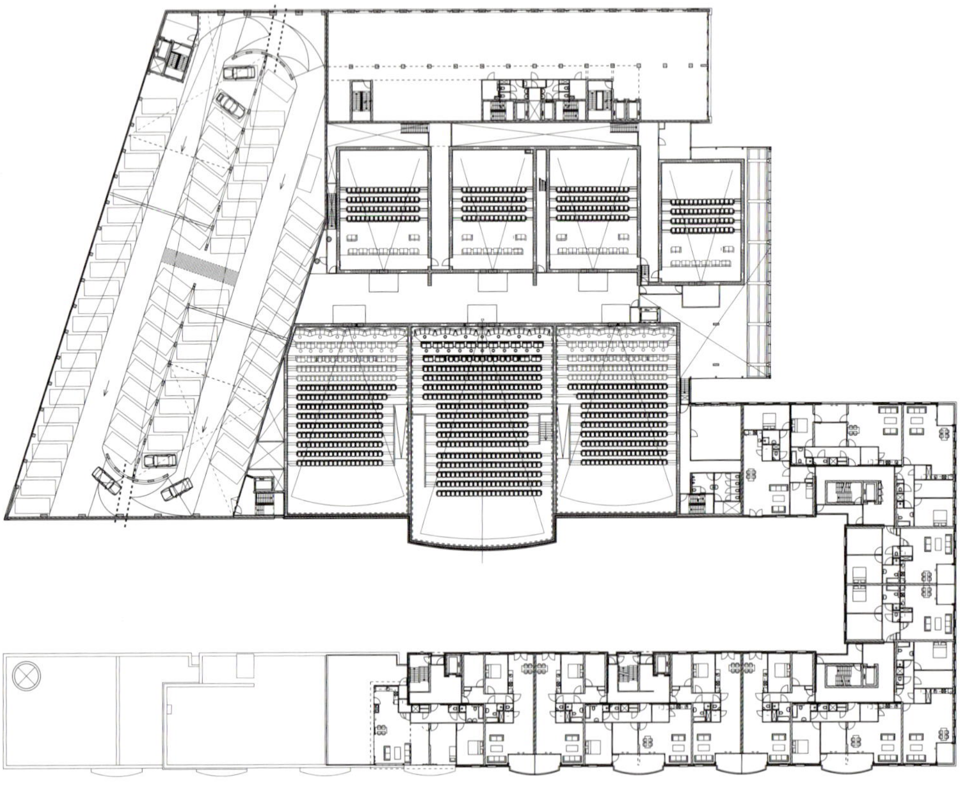

← | **Interior view,** foyer with counter
↓ | **Interior view,** cinema big hall

DP6 architectuurstudio

↑ | **View from steet,** cinema embedded in the sound barrier

CineMec

Ede

Near the Ede exit of the A12 motorway, a new Infotainment Center has been built. The building forms the conclusion of a sound barrier embankment which extends over several kilometers. The red sculptural form of the cinema extends from the sound barrier's grass-covered banks. In order to improve efficiency, the projection rooms – the driving force of the business – are located close together in a single large area on the upper floor. Offices, meeting rooms, and executive rooms have been accommodated in a separate volume which overlooks the activities throughout the building and the entrance lobby.

PROJECT FACTS

Address: Laan der Verenigde Naties 150, 6716 JE Ede, The Netherlands. **Planning partner:** ABT Adviesbureau voor bouwtechniek (structural engineers), Adviesbureau J. van Toorenburg (lighting and heating), DGMR Raadgevende Ingenieurs (building physics). **Client:** CineMec. **Completion:** ongoing. **Additional functions:** sound barrier, infotainment center, congress center, theater. **Main materials:** glass, steel. **Setting:** suburban.

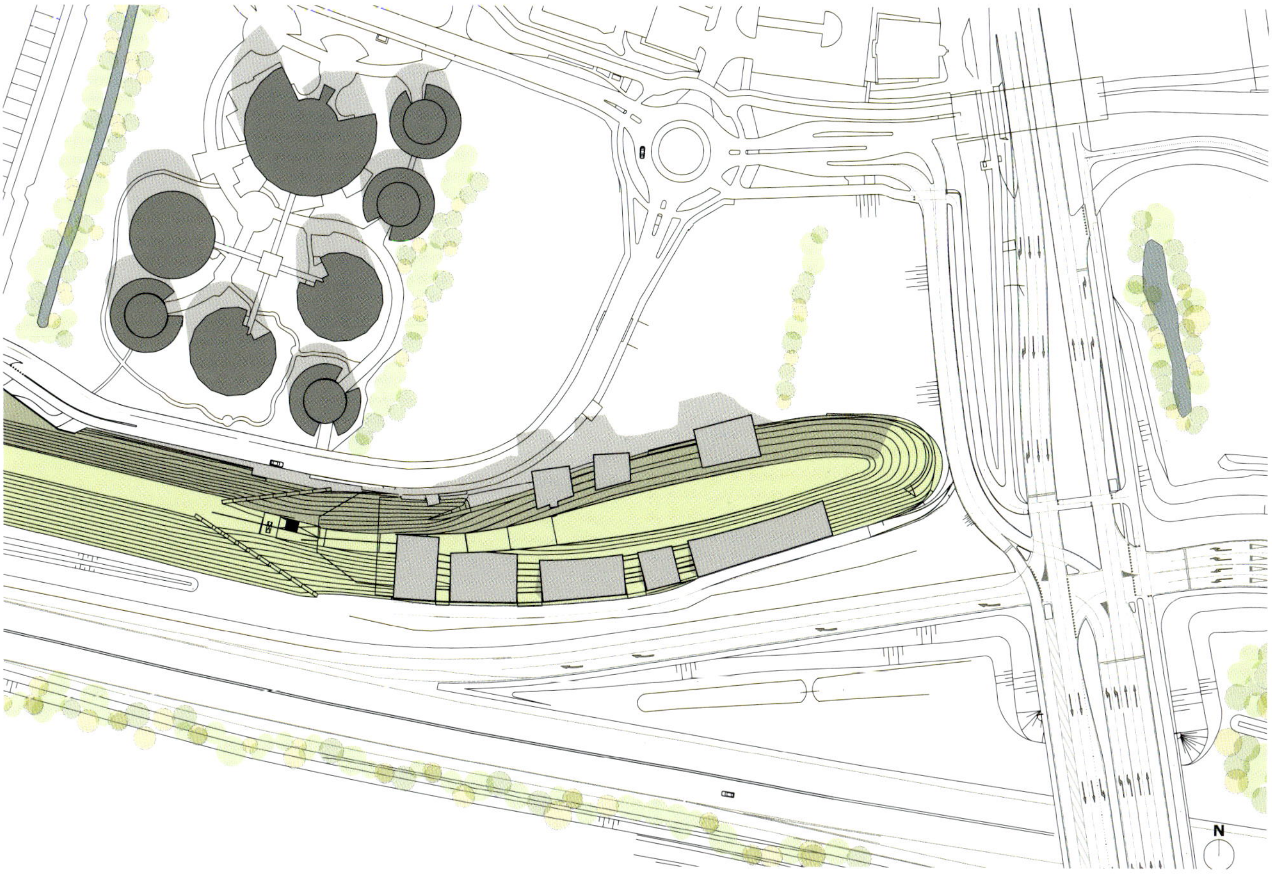

↑ | Site plan

↓ | Entrance area at dusk

meierpartner architekten eth sia ag / Marcel Waltzer, Jeannette Rigaux, Martin Heimgartner, Ulrich Steffen

↑ | Escalator
→ | Foyer

Pathé

Dietlikon

The entry façade of the Ciné Pathé Dietlikon is characterized by a 15-meter high fully glazed hall, which steps slightly out of the volume, and a long projecting marquee placed above it. The dramatic opening offers views inside the building. The foyer lies partially below the theater seat levels and thus receives its individual spatial profile. Using the functionally integrated entry and exit levels, visitors before and after a viewing are led separately back to the foyer. The color scheme of the cinema landscape corresponds to the Pathé corporate identity designed by the Parisian studio Naço.

PROJECT FACTS

Address: Moorstrasse 2, 8304 Dietlikon, Switzerland. **Interior Design:** Naço Paris, Marcelo Joulia. **Client:** Pathé Suisse SA, IKEA Immobilien AG. **Completion:** 2004. **Number of seats:** all audiences: 2,300; main audience: 500. **Largest screen diameter:** 21.65 m. **Sound equipment:** KHS, QSC, Dolby Digital CP 650. **Kind of projection:** Cinémeccanica, Schneider lenses. **Main materials:** exterior: glass façade, metal covering façades; interior: carpet, parquet. **Setting:** suburban.

↑ | **Audience,** red seatings and red carpet
↙ | **Ground floor plan and section**

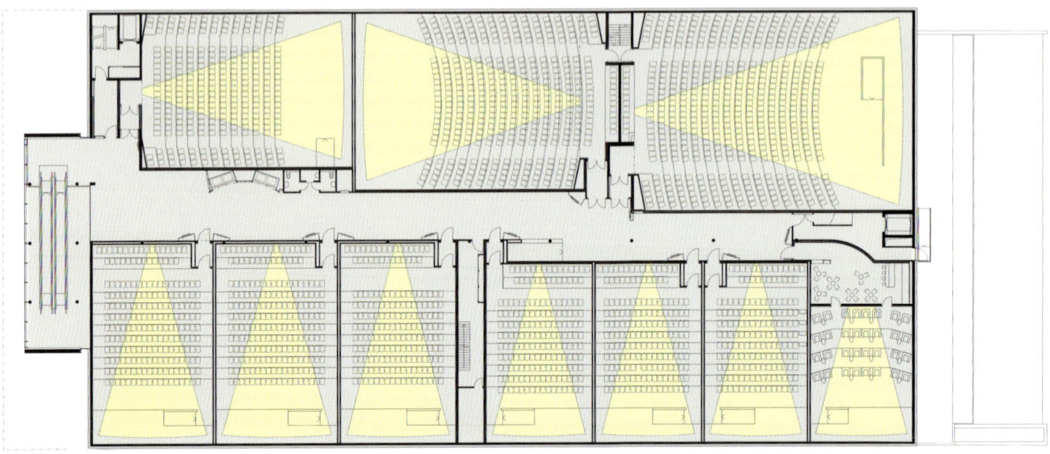

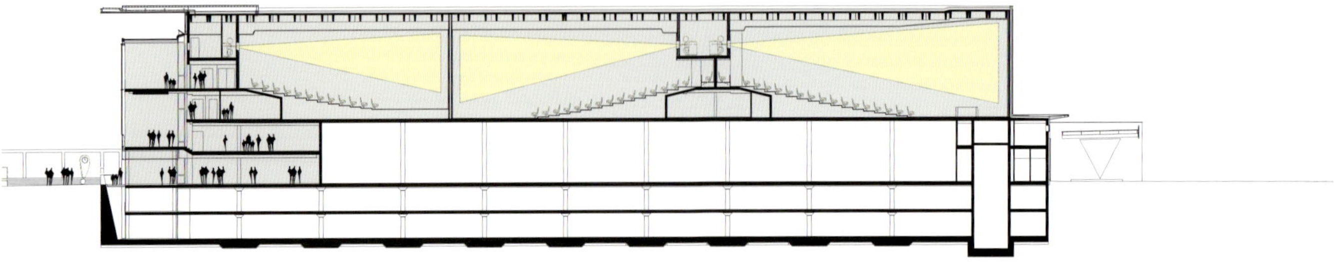

← | **Escalator and seating area**
↙ | **Lounge area** with view to the foyer

meierpartner architekten eth sia ag / Marcel Waltzer, Jeannette Rigaux, Martin Heimgartner, Ulrich Steffen

↑ | **Façade,** by night

Maxx Filmpalast

Emmenbrücke

The ground level of the MaxX Film Palacet in Emmenbrücke houses retail space and a large modern cinema with 8 screens, the first of its kind in Switzerland. The transparent membrane next to the square offers a view of the spacious and colorful machinery of a contemporary cinema operation. The theaters are aligned to either side of a central backbone. A generous, vivacious foyer and amusement areas are found below the sloping cinemas. A suspended entry gangway separates the flow of entering visitors from those leaving the movies only inside the multiplex structure.

PROJECT FACTS

Address: Seetalplatz 1, 6020 Emmenbrücke, Switzerland. **Interior Design:** JOI DESIGN Hamburg. **Client:** Maxx Filmpalast AG (cinema), Bülow AG Switzerland (building), Credit suisse Asset Management. **Completion:** 2000. **Number of seats:** 2,200. **Largest screen diameter:** 23,5 m. **Sound equipment:** Dolby Digital / THX Saal 3. **Kind of projection:** Kinoton. **Additional functions:** shopping center, gastronomy. **Main materials:** exterior: glass, metal; interior: stone, carpet, wood floor. **Setting:** urban.

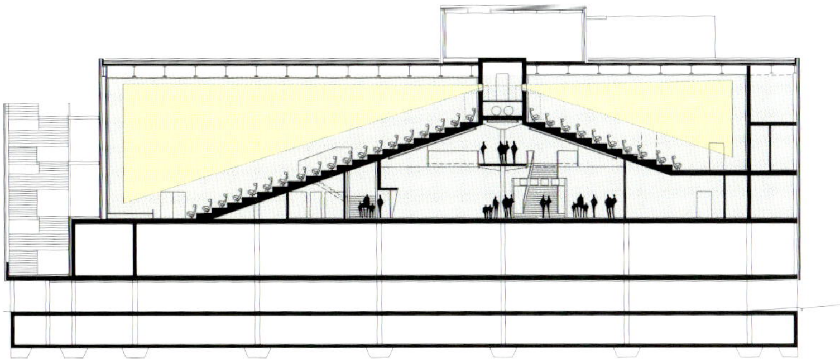

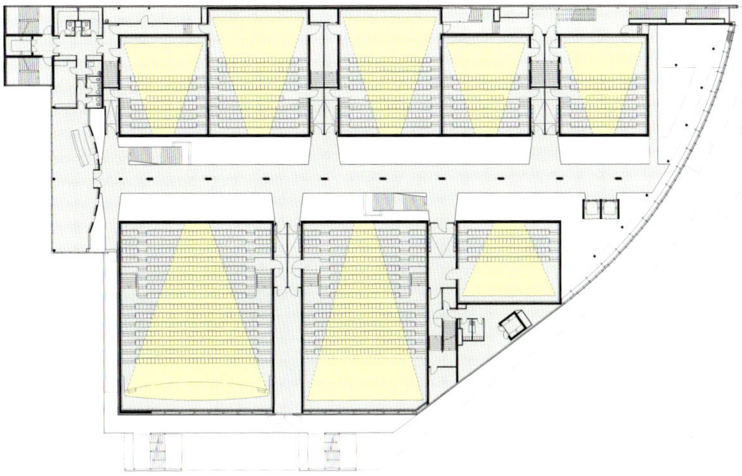

↑↑ | Section
↑ | Second floor plan

↑ | Foyer
↓ | Exterior view

meierpartner architekten eth sia ag / Marcel Waltzer, Jeannette Rigaux, Martin Heimgartner, Ulrich Steffen

↑ | **Foyer,** cashpoint
↗ | **View through the foyer**
→ | **Entrance** to audience 10

Pathé Westside

Berne

Cinéma Pathé Westside offers a 2,400 capacity in 11 cinemas. The center's architecture carries the unmistakable signature of Daniel Libeskind, and the cinema has been organized using his concept of form. The inner functional needs of the multiplex cinema were adjusted to Libeskind's architectural poise, especially in the area of the foyer. The variegated communications system and the orthogonal theater geometry still create a clearly independent vocabulary attuned to the specifics of cinema operation. The color design of the cinema landscape corresponds to the Pathé corporate identity, designed by the Parisian studio Naço.

PROJECT FACTS

Address: Riedbachstrasse 102, 3027 Berne, Switzerland. **Planning partner:** overall project Westside: Daniel Libeskind. **Interior Design:** Naço Paris, Marcelo Joulia. **Client:** Pathé Suisse SA, ARGE TU Westside Rhomberg Bau AG, Strabag AG. **Completion:** 2008. **Number of seats:** all audiences 2,400; main audience: 500. **Largest screen diameter:** 22.45 m. **Sound equipment:** KHS, Crown, Dolby Digital CP 650. **Kind of projection:** Cinemeccanica, Schneider lenses. **Setting:** suburban.

↑ | Audience

↙ | Ground floor plan

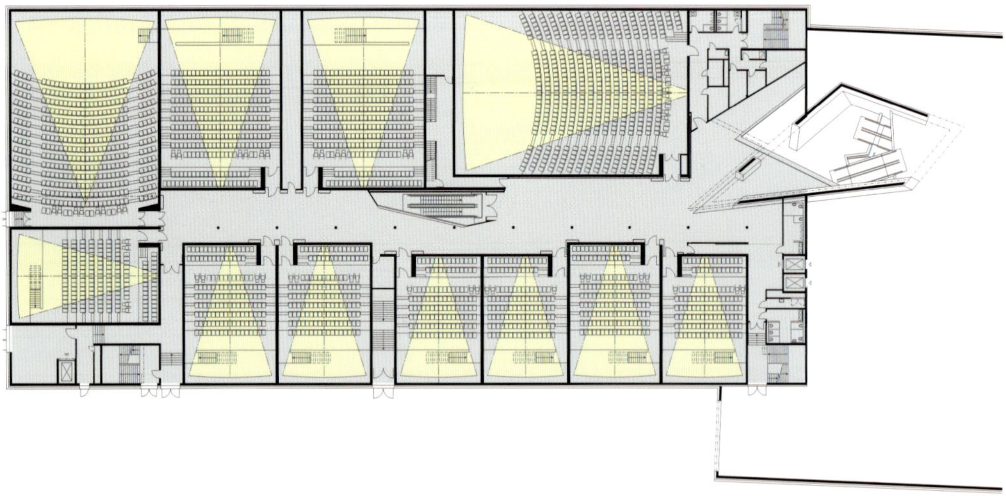

← | **Worm's-eye view,** view to gallery
↙ | **Gallery**
↓ | **Site plan,** by Daniel Libeskind

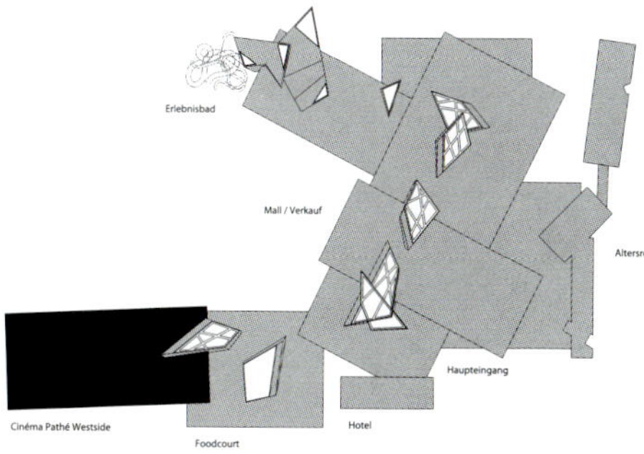

ATP Architekten und Ingenieure

↑ | **Exterior view** by night
→ | **Interior view,** escalator

Centrum Cerny Most

Praha

Centrum Cerny Most came about in the 1990s as the first shopping, office and amusement center in the Czech Republic. The five-story "closed box" building, which may be accessed from several levels, is found behind the glazed atrium measuring 14 by 25 meters housing escalators und elevators. Rental spaces for a furniture store, a health center, restaurants and shops are found on the three below-street levels. The "Village Cinemas" multiplex with 12 screens and a total capacity for 2,000 visitors takes up the fourth and fifth floors. To allow a possible third use of the cinema area, the architects built only the empty building envelope, which was filled with steel structures on its interior by the operator.

PROJECT FACTS

Address: Nákupní centrum, Chlumecká 765/6, Praha 9, Czech Republic. **Client:** Intershop Prag / RODAMCO. **Completion:** 2000. **Number of seats:** 2,000. **Setting:** peripheral.

↑ | **Façade** by night
← | **Stairs and escalators**
↓ | **Plan**

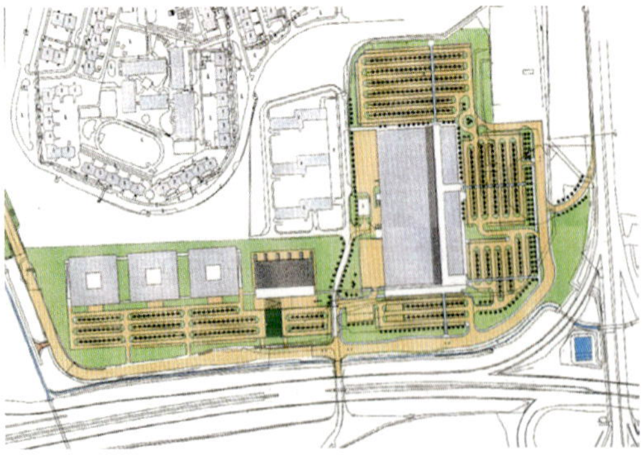

← | View into the atrium
↓ | Rear façade

ATP Architekten und Ingenieure

↑ | **Covered plaza,** urban center making different building features perceivable
→ | **Bird's-eye view,** atrium by night

UCI Kinowelt Millennium City

Vienna

One of the largest urban entertainment centers in whole Europe came about as an addition to the Millennium Towers on the Danube banks. The complex features a multiplex cinema for 3,800 visitors, a fitness center, a dance temple, a conference center, as well as restaurants and shopping. The two-story shopping center located in the Millennium Tower's base is connected via a 14 meter-high glazed plaza on the top level and an adjacent mall on the ground level. Four solid towers of natural stone support the glass block of the plaza. From the urban planning perspective, they repeat the motifs of the historic bock structures and indicate the start of the rising momentum of the three-dimensionally modeled wave of the aluminum roof. Two large spaces with views over Vienna were created directly below.

PROJECT FACTS

Address: Wehlistraße 66, 1200 Vienna, Austria. **Client:** Aurora Bauprojekt GmbH. **Completion:** 2001. **Number of seats:** main audience: 747. **Largest screen diameter:** 27 m. **Sound equipment:** DTS, Dolby Digital, SRD, SDDS, Dolby Digital EX-System. **Setting:** urban.

↑ | **Premiere cinema,** screen 4
← | **Site plan**

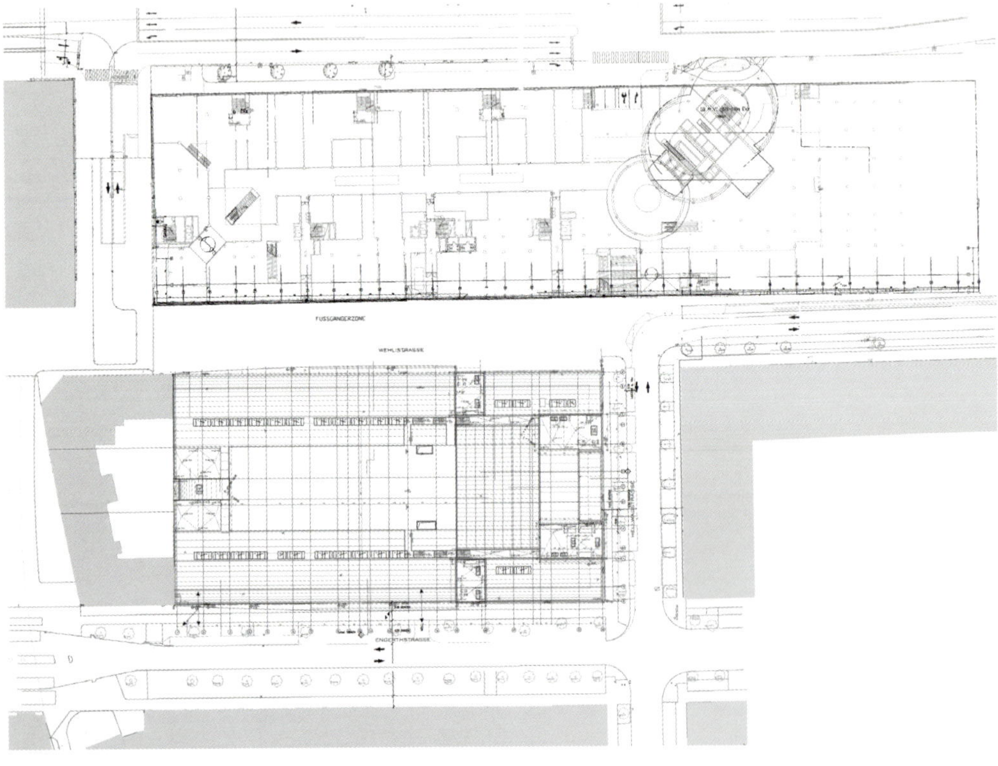

← | Sketches
↓ | Atrium from galerie

Aedas Architects Limited

↑ I **Foyer**
→ I **Ticket Sales Counter**

12 Screen Cinema De Lux

Derby

Offering twelve screens on its five floors, this cinema was constructed in only 35 weeks' time. The requirement of the surrounding shopping center to remain open during the process presented a challenge. In addition to the twelve screens, which include two VIP screens, the complex houses several other functions: rooms for private hire, bars and restaurants. The cinema is connected to the shopping center by escalators and passenger lifts. Each screen and room displays a distinctive design achieved with a combination of illumination, choice of materials and furniture selection in accordance to its function and size.

PROJECT FACTS

Address: Westfield Shopping Centre, Derby DE1 2PQ, United Kingdom. **Planning partners:** Derby City Council. **Client:** National Amusements USA. **Completion:** 2008. **Number of seats:** 2,332. **Largest screen diameter:** 15.44 m. **Sound equipment:** CP650 cinema sound processor with excrown amplifiers. **Kind of projection:** Century 35 mm projector. **Additional functions:** shopping center. **Setting:** inner city.

↑ | Chatter's Bar
← | Director's Auditorium

← | **Director's Lounge**

↓ | **Floor plan level 4,** cinema, auditoria and foyer

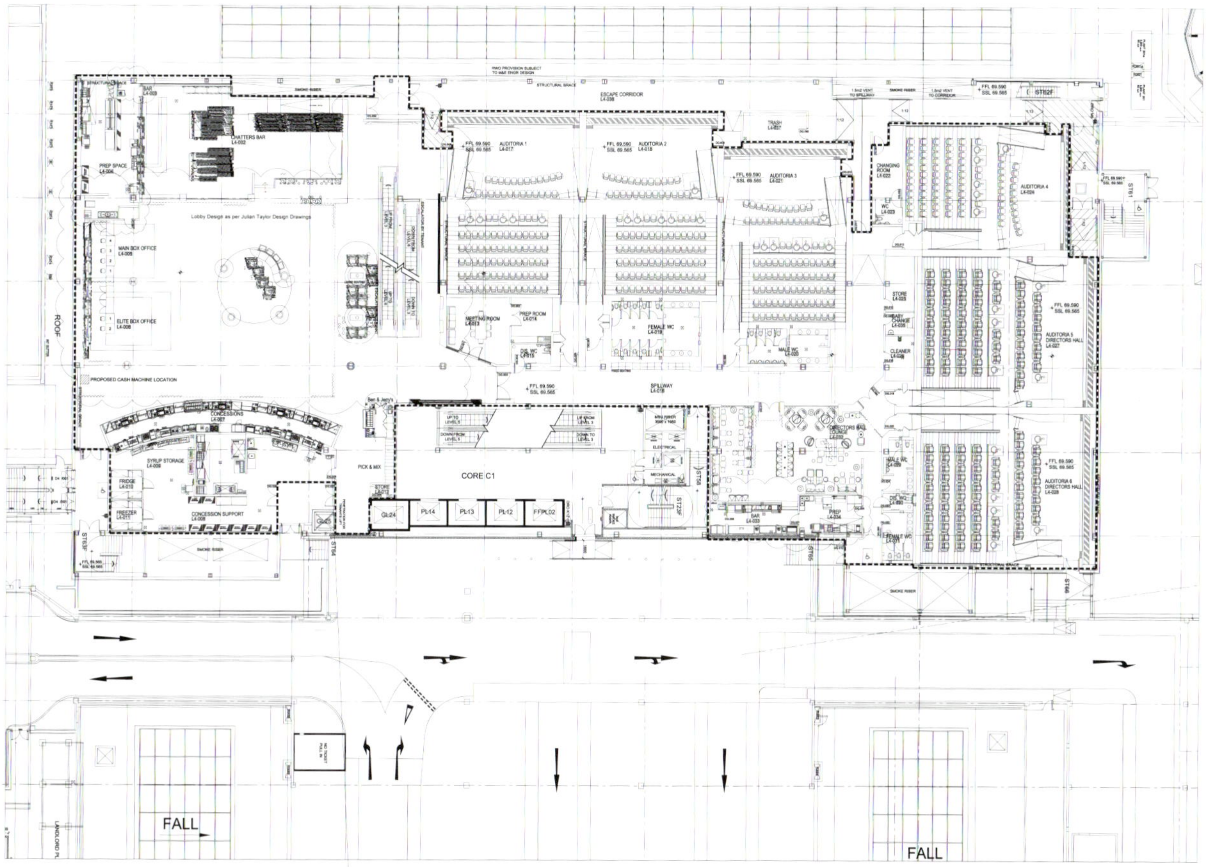

Index

Arch

itects Index

5+1AA

Via Interiano 3/11
16124 Genova (Italy)
T +39.010.540095
F +39.010.5702094
info@5piu1aa.com
www.5piu1aa.com

→ **152**

AEDAS ARCHITECTS LIMITED

St Mary's Court, 21 St Mary's Street
Shrewsbury SY1 1ED (United Kingdom)
T +44.174.3263000
F +44.174.3232717
london@aedas.com
www.aedas.com

→ **242**

Atelier Aires Mateus

Rua Silva Carvalho, 175 r/c
1250-250 Lisboa (Portugal)
T +351.21.3815650
F+ 351.21.3815659
m@airesmateus.com
www.airesmateus.com

→ **176**

arb Architekten

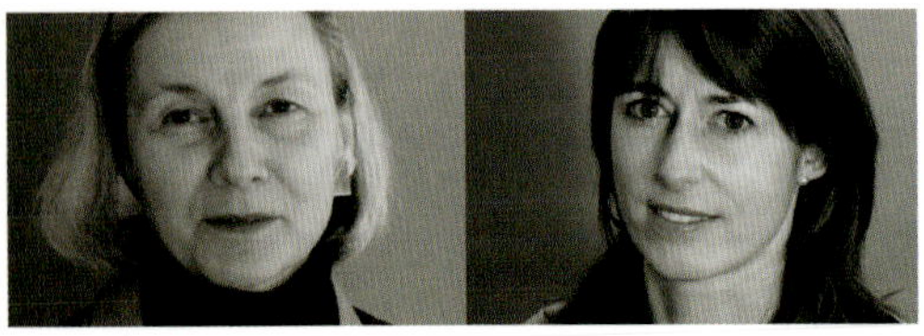

Brunnadernstrasse 28b
3006 Berne (Switzerland)
T +41.31.3516002
F +41.31.3511403
arb@arb.ch
www.arb.ch

→ **104**

Arris Architects

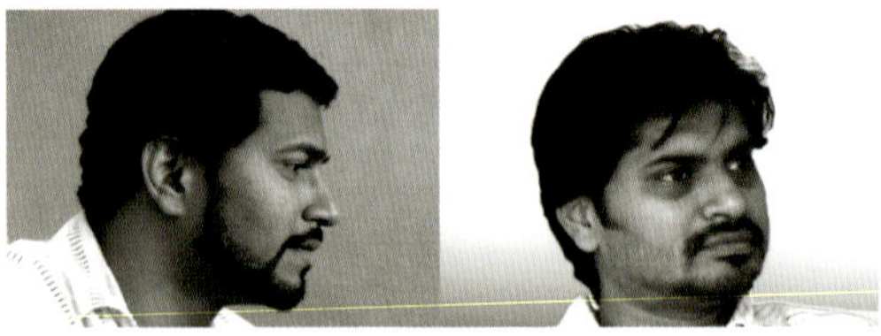

2nd level, Saro-Darshan Towers, Adjacent to M.H. School
Thane West Maharashtra 400 602 (India)
T +91.22.25390609
F +91.22.254339.85
arris@arris-architects.com
www.arris-architects.com

→ **204, 210, 214**

Atelier de l'Île

3 rue Dagorno
75012 Paris (France)
T +33.1.48062200
F +33.1.48069175
archi@atile.fr

→ **194**

ATP Architekten und Ingenieure

Franziskanerstraße 14
81669 Munich (Germany)
T +49.89.455620
info_muc@atp.ag
www.atp.ag

→ **200, 234, 238**

Avery Associates Architects

270 Vauxhall Bridge road
London SW1V 1BB (United Kingdom)
T +44.20.72336262
F +44.20.72335182
enquiries@avery-architects.co.uk
www.avery-architects.co.uk

→ **68**

Franklin Azzi Architecture

2, rue d' hauteville
75010 Paris (Francc)
T +33.1.40266821
F +33.1.42467389
info@franklinazzi.com
www.franklinazzi.com

→ **32, 146**

bad architects group

Jahnstraße 14
6020 Innsbruck (Austria)
T +43.512.5617270
F +43.512.5617272
welcome@bad-architects.gp
www.bad-architects.gp

→ **120**

Belzberg Architects

1507 20th Street, Suite C
Santa Monica, CA 90404 (USA)
T +1.310.4539611
F +1.310.4539166
belzbergarchitects@gmail.com
www.belzbergarchitects.com

→ 114

Architect Maarten Douwe Bredero

Kortestraat 27
7419 CK Deventer (The Netherlands)
T +31.570.645458
F +31.570.645085
mail@architectmaartendouwebredero.com
www.architectmaartendouwebredero.com

→ 86

BURO II

Hoogleedsesteenweg 415
8800 Roeselare (Belgium)
T +51.21.1105
F +51.22.4674
info@buro2.be
www.buro2.be

→ 28

BWM Architekten und Partner

Margaretenplatz 4/L1
1050 Vienna (Austria)
T +43.1.2059070
F +43.1.205907020
office@bwm.at
www.bwm.at

→ 122

Chapman Taylor Czech Republic

Jilska 4
110 00 Praha 1 (Czech Republic)
T +420.2.24214121
F +420.2.24214122
ctprague@chapmantaylor.cz
www.chapmantaylor.com

→ 74

Code Unique Architekten

Katharinenstraße 5
01099 Dresden (Germany)
T +49.351.81078800
F +49.351.81078825
contact@codeunique.de
www.codeunique.de

→ 34

Derlot Pty. ltd.

Unit 3/15 Edmondstone Street
West End Brisbane, Qld 4101 (Australia)
T +61.404682139
info@derlot.com
www.derlot.com

→ 110

DP6 architectuurstudio

Prof. Snijdersstraat 5
2628 RA Delft (The Netherlands)
T +31.15.2120110
F +31.15.2144822
info@dp6.nl
www.dp6.nl

→ 56, 222

DTA Architects

22 Wicklow Street
Dublin 2 (Ireland)
T +353.1.6777742
F +353.1.6777713
info@dta.ie
www.dta.ie

→ 16

Fletcher Priest Architects

Middlesex House, 34/42 Cleveland Street
London, W1T 4JE (United Kingdom)
T +44.20.70342200
F +44.20.76375347
london@fletcherpriest.com
www.fletcherpriest.com

→ 70, 182

Frei + Saarinen Architekten

Agnesstrasse 2
8004 Zurich (Switzerland)
T +41.43.2052136
F +41.43.2052136
info@freisaarinen.ch
www.freisaarinen.ch

→ 64

Freyrie & Pestalozza Architetti Associati

Via Pietrasanta 14
20147 Milano (Italy)
T +39.02.5660961
F +39.02.56816940
fparchitetti@fparchitetti.it
www.fparchitetti.it

→ 50

architectenbureau Fritz

Postbus 141
1400 AC Bussum (The Netherlands)
T +31.35.6920975
F +31.35.6921629
post@bureaufritz.nl
www.bureaufritz.nl

→ 168

Gensler, Washington DC

8633 Colesville Road
Silver Spring, MD 20910 (USA)
T +1.301.4956720
F +1.301.4956777
info@gensler.com
www.gensler.com

→ 24

Henket & partners architecten

Postbus 2126
5260 CC Vught (The Netherlands)
T +31.411.601618
F +31.411.601887
info@henket.nl
www.henket.nl

→ 180

Günter Hermann Architekten

Sophienstraße 17
70178 Stuttgart (Germany)
T +49.711.607740
F +49.711.6077444
stuttgart@gharchitekten.de
www.gharchitekten.de

→ 42

Steven Holl Architects

450 W. 31st Street, 11th floor,
New York, NY 10001 (USA)
T +1.212.6297262
F +1.212.6297312
mail@stevenholl.com
www.stevenholl.com

→ 112

Hopkins Architects and Expedition Engineers

27 Broadley Terrace
London NW1 6LG (United Kingdom)
T +44.20.77241751
F +44.20.77230932
mail@hopkins.co.uk
www.hopkins.co.uk

→ 128

Atelier Feichang Jianzhu

Yuan Ming Yuan East Gate Nei,Yard No.1 on northside,
Yuan Ming Yuan Dong Lu,
Beijing, 100084 (China)
T +86.10.82622712
F +86.10.82622712
fcjz@fcjz.com
www.fcjz.com

→ 124

Kaup + Wiegand Architekten BDA

Mommsenstraße 57
10629 Berlin (Germany)
T +49.30.446.2126
F +49.30.446.2936
info@kaupwiegand.de
www.kaupwiegand.de

→ 98

Kraaijvanger.Urbis

Watertorenweg 336
3063 HA Rotterdam (The Netherlands)
T +31.10.4989292
F +31.10.4989200
mail@kraaijvanger.urbis.nl
www.kraaijvanger.urbis.nl

→ 218

James Law Cybertecture International Ltd.

402-3, InnoCentre, 72 Tat Chee Avenue,
Kowloon Tong, Hong Kong (China)
T +852.238.19997
hongkong@jameslawcybertecture.com
www.jameslawcybertecture.com

→ 46

Lehrecke Architekten BDA

Lärchenweg 33
14055 Berlin (Germany)
T +49.30.3025353
F +49.30.3029291
lehrecke-architekten@t-online.de

→ 186

Lorenz & Partner GmbH

Albert-Einstein-Ring 19
22761 Hamburg (Germany)
T +49.40.8195190
F +49.40.81951950
info@lorenzHH.de
www.lorenzHH.de

→ 102

Architekturbüro [lu:p]

Ringstraße 21
96271 Grub am Forst (Germany)
T +49.9560.8122
F +49.9560.8121
info@lu-p.de
www.lu-p.de

→ 38

Robert Majkut Design

Ul. Widok 8
00-023 Warsaw (Poland)
T +48.22.6906464
F +48.22.6906463
studio@design.pl
www.design.pl

→ 60, 78

meierpartner architekten eth sia ag

Kantonsschulstrasse 6
8620 Wetzikon (Switzerland)
T +41.44.9330505
F +41.44.9330506
info@mparch.ch
www.mparch.ch

→ 224, 228, 230

Bureau des Mésarchitectures

62, rue Tiquetonne
75002 Paris (France)
T +33.1.40280048
F +33.1.40280049
bureau@mesarchitecture.com
www.mesarchitecture.org

→ 118

Muungano

Dr. Abelins gata 3K
118 53 Stockholm (Sweden)
T +46.708.853998
info@muungano.com
www.muungano.com

→ 160

Sergei Tchoban Architekt BDA, nps tchoban voss, A. M. Prasch S. Tchoban E. Voss

Rosenthaler Straße 40/41
10178 Berlin (Germany)
T +49.30.2839200
F +49.30.283920200
berlin@npstv.de
www.npstv.de

→ 12

OMA – Office for Metropolitan Architecture

Heer Bokelweg 149
3032 AD Rotterdam (The Netherlands)
T +31.10.2438200
F +31.10.2438202
office@oma.com
www.oma.nl

→ 158

Page + Steele, IBI Group Architects

95 St. Clair Avenue West Suite 200
Toronto, ON M4V1N6, (Canada)
T +1.416.9249966
F +1.416.9249067
pagesteele.info@ibigroup.com
www.pagesteele.com

→ 88

Atelier Christian de Portzamparc

1, rue de l'Aude
75014 Paris (France)
T +33.1.43271197
F +33.1.43277479
studio@chdeportzamparc.com
www.chdeportzamparc.com

→ 20

Riepl Riepl Architekten

OK Platz 1A
4020 Linz (Austria)
T +43.732.782300
F +43.732.78230010
arch@rieplriepl.com
www.rieplriepl.com

→ 172

Rojkind Arquitectos

Campos Eliseos 432
col. Polanco, (Mexico)
T +52.55.52808369
F +52.55.52808021
www.rojkindarquitectos.com

→ 164

RTKL

2101 L Street, Suite 200,
Washington, DC 20037 (USA)
T +1.202.8334400
F +1.202.8875168
xliu@rtkl.com
RTKL.com

→ 138

schmidt hammer lassen architects

Aaboulevarden 37,5
8000 Aarhus C (Denmark)
T +45.86.201900
F +45.86.184513
info@shl.dk
www.shl.dc

→ 142

Detlev Schneider

Virchowstraße 17 a
90409 Nuremberg (Germany)
T +49.911.518340
F +49.911.5183431
info@detlevschneider.de
www.detlevschneider.de

→ 184

SERERO Architects

136 Avenue Parmentier
75011 Paris (France)
T +33.1.45081431
F +33.1.53010955
info@serero.com
www.serero.com

→ 148

Soeters Van Eldonk architecten

Postbus 15550
1001 NB Amsterdam (The Netherlands)
T +31.20.6242939
F +31.20.6246928
communicatie@soetersvaneldonk.nl
www.soetersvaneldonk.nl

→ 82, 154

Steinmayr & Mascher

Büro Steinmayr:
Neustadt 5
6800 Feldkirch (Austria)
T +43.552.271301
F +43.552.27130120

Büro Mascher:
Untere Zeile 14
3482 Gösing am Wagram (Austria)
T +43.273.877085
F +43.699.13511441

office@steinmayr.com
www.steinmayr-mascher.com

→ 134

The Jerde Partnership, Inc.

913 Ocean Front Walk,
Venice, CA 90291 (USA)
T +1.310.3991987
F +1.310.3921316
busdev@jerde.com
www.jerde.com

→ 208

Studio Ramin Visch

Groenhoedenveem 18
1019 BL Amsterdam (The Netherlands)
T +31.20.6710902
F +31.20.7781620
office@raminvisch.nl
www.raminvisch.com

→ **52**

Andrea Viviani Architects

Via Eremitano 12
35138 Padova (Italy)
T +39.049.661461
F +39.049.661461
a.viviani@awn.it
www.andreaviviani.it

→ **92, 94**

Wallrath & Weinert Architekten

Georgstraße 15
50676 Cologne (Germany)
T +49.221.2409139
F +49.221.2409169
info@ww-architects.de
www.ww-architects.de

→ **190**

Ackermans, Guy 223
De architekten Cie. 9 b.
Avery, Bryan 68, 69
Axelsen, Frank – Fotolia.com 108, 109
Baan, Iwan 113 a.
Bolk, Florian 12–14
Borel, Nicolas 20–23
Bosco, Emil / Viviani Architects 94–97
Bourdeille, Julien and Csajko, Patrick / le studio production 230–233
Boxtel, Simon van 52 (portrait)
Bradley, John 182 (portrait)
Brine, Richard 128–131
Brünjes, Wolfgang 102
Chan, Benny of Fotoworks 114–117
Coop Himmelb(l)au 8. m. a.
Dieguez / Fridman 164–167
Frydrysiak, Maciej 60–63
G F Holding Ltd. 242–245
Gascoigne, Chris 182, 183
Gericke, Wolf-Dieter 42–45
Gigler, Dominik 158 (portrait)
Gonzales Buzzio, Andres Rodrigo – Fotolia.com 132, 133
Groehn, Florian 110, 111
Hadid, Zaha Architects 9 a.
Hat Productions 86 (portrait)
He, Shu 113 b. l+r, 124–126
Heckmann, Uli 164 (portrait)
Heitoff, Mark 112 (portrait)
Helbling, Andrea / Arazebra Fotografien 228, 229
Henz, Hannes 64–67
isochrom.com 9 b.
Jantscher, Thomas / ATP 200–203
Josef Herfert / ATP 238–241
Jungmann, Ales / ATP 234–237
Kavanagh, Ros 16–19
Kawano, Hiroyuki 208, 209
Keller, Thomas 104–107
Kierok, Thomas 98–101
Kievits, Michel 218–221
Klomfar, Bruno 134–137
Kohler, Carola 190–193
ktsdesign – Fotolia.com 10, 11
Kuijvenhoven, Wilma 168–171
Lai, Chun Photography 24–27
Lejona, Andres 118, 119
Lintner, Linus 186, 187 a., 188, 189
Lorenz, Renee 38–41
Lukkien 222
Malhão, Daniel 176–179
Maritati, Giuseppe 152 (portrait)
Mesman, Rene 52
Meuser, Philipp 12 (portrait)
Mølvig, Thomas 142–145
Muciaccia, Alberto / VivianiArchitects 92, 93
Musch, Jeroen 53–57
Narr, Robert 224, 227
Neutlings Riedijk Architects 8 m. b.
Nijkerk, Jurriaan 86, 87
Norman, Sally Anne / Gateshead 70–73
Öhlund, Sanna 160 (portrait)
Olo Studio 78–81
Pausch, Josef 172–175
pdesign – Fotolia.com 198, 199
Pesarini Studio 50, 51
Pugliese, Joe 208 (portrait)
Ricciotti, R. & 5+1AA 152, 153
Richters, Christian 58, 59
Scagliola, Daria & Brakkee, Stijn 82–85, 154–157
Silva, Jorge P 176 (portrait)
Sit, Andrew 88
Soltmannowski, Cristoph Medienbüro+ Kommunikation 225, 226
Stanger / ATP 200, 234, 238 (portraits)
Steiner, Rupert 122, 123
Timmer, Ingmar 82, 154 (portraits)
Tompsett, Clive 160–163
UCI KINOWELT Millennium City 240
Uffelen, Chris van 6, 8 a., 15, 187 b.
Vandamme, Kris 28–31
Voeten, S. Fotografie 180, 181
Weber, Wolfram / CineCittá Multiplexkino, Nuremberg 184, 185
Xing, Fu 127, 138–141
Xu, David 88 (portrait)
Zapf, Michael 103 a
Zerkaulen, M. 194–197

All other pictures, especially portraits and plans, were made available by the architects.

Cover front: Ros Kavanagh (Light House Cinema by DTA Architects / Dermot Reynolds, Colin Mackay)
Cover back: left and right: Olo Studio (Multikino Golden Terraces by Robert Majkut Design)

The Deutsche Bibliothek is registering this publication in the Deutsche Nationalbibliographie; detailed bibliographical information can be found on the Internet at http://dnb.ddb.de

ISBN 978-3-03768-027-8

1st edition 2009

Editorial staff: Marek Heinel
Translation: Alice Bayandin, Cosima Talhouni
Graphic concept: ON Grafik | Tom Wibberenz
Layout: Natascha Saupe, Georgia van Uffelen
Reproduction: Bild1Druck GmbH, Berlin